WikiLeaking

Recent Releases from Open Court

1984 and Philosophy: Is Resistance Futile?
Edited by Ezio Di Nucci and Stefan Storrie

The Handmaid's Tale and Philosophy: A Womb of One's Own
Edited by Rachel Robison-Greene

Scott Adams and Philosophy: A Hole in the Fabric of Reality
Edited by Daniel Yim, Galen Foresman, and Robert Arp

The Americans and Philosophy: Reds in the Bed
Edited by Robert Arp and Kevin Guilfoy

The X-Files and Philosophy: The Truth Is In Here
Edited by Robert Arp

The Man in the High Castle and Philosophy: Subversive Reports from Another Reality
Edited by Bruce Krajewski and Joshua Heter

For full details of all Open Court books, visit www.opencourtbooks.com.

WikiLeaking

The Ethics of Secrecy and Exposure

EDITED BY

CHRISTIAN COTTON AND ROBERT ARP

OPEN COURT
Chicago

To find out more about Open Court books, visit our website at www.opencourtbooks.com.

Open Court Publishing Company is a division of Carus Publishing Company, dba Cricket Media.

Copyright © 2019 by Carus Publishing Company, dba Cricket Media

First printing 2019

Printed and bound in the United States of America.

WikiLeaking: The Ethics of Secrecy and Exposure

ISBN: 978-0-8126-9988-3

Library of Congress Control Number: 2018959070

This book is also available as an e-book (ISBN 978-0-8126-9997-5).

Document Archive

About

CHRISTIAN COTTON

Secrets.

Everybody has them. For the most part, they're personal and harmless. But, often enough, they're not. When those secrets are held and guarded by powerful institutions and organizations in both public and private sectors—government agencies and departments, transnational corporations, non-governmental organizations (NGO's), supranational economic institutions—whose reach and influence affect millions, or even billions, of people, often without their knowledge or consent, we face a much different scenario. At that point, it becomes a matter of ethical importance. As the philosophical study of right and wrong action, good and bad character, just and unjust institutions, *ethics* brings a substantial weight to the question of just when, if ever, secrecy is appropriate.

Harry S. Truman once remarked, "Secrecy and a free, democratic government don't mix." This from the man who presided over the creation of the CIA. Some years later, speaking before the American Newspaper Publishers Association in late April, 1961, John F. Kennedy proclaimed, "The very word 'secrecy' is repugnant in a free and open society." This from the man who had—just three weeks earlier—approved the CIA-sponsored covert invasion of the Bay of Pigs, and only a week prior had seen that mission—

to overthrow Fidel Castro's Communist regime—fail. You might get the feeling that you're being told a "noble lie" here, an official narrative of transparency that belies an official policy of secrecy. You might even think it's a con game.

So, when does the level of secrecy cross the proverbial line, and when is the exposure of those secrets ethically justified? We all know the familiar justifications offered by these large, powerful groups to keep their secrets. "It's for your own good" or "It's a matter of national security" or "That's need to know, and *you* don't need to know." Well, what *do* we need to know? Everyone's entitled to a bit of secrecy, but sometimes those secrets involve other people and involve them in ways that violate their rights. So, what *do* we have a right to know? What's the place of transparency and accountability in a "free and open" society? And, what are the risks of exposure, and are they risks worth taking?

Enter WikiLeaks.

In a 2017 interview with Sean Hannity, WikiLeaks founder Julian Assange asserted, "The best type of government comes from a government that is scrutinized by the people when they have true information about our governments, major corporations, other power actors in society." As a watchdog media outlet, WikiLeaks prides itself on adhering to the strong principles of transparency and accountability. It's become famous—and *infamous*—for its release of huge caches of unredacted original documents detailing the illegal, extra-legal, and unethical activities of numerous governments, corporations, and other organizations. Documents are sent to WikiLeaks by sources via a secure dropbox that ensures their anonymity.

But, if the risks to leakers who share their information with WikiLeaks are minimized by their anonymity (even to WikiLeaks), the risks of exposure to those powerful actors are not. Nor are the risks to otherwise innocent individuals and groups contained in those unredacted documents, who are exposed just as those in power are exposed. And, we can't overlook the risks to WikiLeaks itself and its staff as the platform that brings this damaging information to the public's eye. This is risky business, and we'd be fools not to consider whether all of this is really *worth* the risks involved. Even if we expose the powers that be—catch them with their pants down—the fallout for others may be severe. This is something that Assange himself knows all too well.

Assange has been holed up in the Ecuadorian Embassy in London, England, where he sought asylum in June of 2012 following a series of legal challenges over allegations of sexual assault in Sweden. Those allegations have since been dropped, but he still faces arrest in the UK for jumping bail and faces possible extradition to the US regarding alleged interference in the 2016 Presidential campaign. In March of 2018, the Ecuadorian government severed Assange's Internet access, effectively cutting him off from the outside world. Since that time, reports of failing health, possible removal of asylum by the government of Ecuador, and the continued worry over possible extradition to the US have kept both Assange and WikiLeaks in the headlines. Assange has officially stepped down as editor-in-chief of WikiLeaks.

Yet, despite all of Assange's personal and professional troubles, WikiLeaks continues its practice of releasing both compromising and controversial information like the recent Vault 7 dump of thousands of CIA internal documents, detailing the agency's software capabilities to perform electronic surveillance and cyber warfare and its ability to compromise operating systems such as Microsoft Windows, macOS, and Linux, as well as cars, smart TVs, web browsers, and the operating systems of most smartphones. WikiLeaks understands the risks, but it's undaunted in its commitment to the principles of transparency and accountability which it believes require that the secrets of these powerful institutions be exposed to public scrutiny.

Though it's not the final word on the ethics of secrecy and exposure, nor on the moral status of WikiLeaks, later in that 2017 interview with Sean Hannity, Assange sums up what he's proud of as editor of WikiLeaks:

I am very proud of three things. Number one, we have never got it wrong in terms of what we say. A document is what it is. Number two, we have never revealed one of our sources ever. Number three, what are we proud of? We are proud that there is not a single instance of anyone coming into physical harm as a result of our publication.

The information is accurate, the sources are protected, and no one is harmed by the release. To borrow a baseball metaphor, that's a perfect batting average.

The debate doesn't end there. WikiLeaks has many critics, both harsh and mild. It also has many defenders, both enthusiastic and tentative.

The chapters that follow reflect these varying shades of opinion about WikiLeaks. The volume itself takes no position; the authors disagree. Yet all these chapters are thought-provoking and raise fascinating questions.

First Dump

Leaky Ship

1
Conspiracies and the Power of WikiLeaks

PETER LUDLOW

Before Julian Assange became the infamous figure we know today, he authored a series of philosophical essays in which he made the case for a culture of leaking secrets. Those papers take the reader on a journey through some abstract concepts in the theory of networks and introduce unfamiliar ideas like "emergent conspiracies" and "cognitive taxes."

Assange's philosophical journey is well worth taking. But, while the journey may be worth taking, it's not an easy one. The way Assange frames his argument leaves it to readers to connect the dots. So let's connect them.

What Are Conspiracies?

One of the core goals of Assange's project has been to dismantle what he calls "conspiracies." For Assange, this isn't the usual sense of conspiracy, with people sitting around in a room plotting some crime or deception. According to Assange's view, it's entirely possible that there could be a conspiracy in which no person involved in the conspiracy is aware that they're part of that conspiracy. But, how is this even possible?

Suppose that you have some information that's valuable—let's say you have some inside information about the financial state of a corporation. That information, like a strong hand at poker, could be made more valuable if you play it correctly.

Here's one way to maximize the value of the information you have: You could seek out someone to trade the information with; let's say you informally swap your information for new information. In this case, you want to be sure the person you're trading with will distribute your information narrowly so that it remains valuable (once the information is broadcast widely it loses most of its value). That person may then trade your information with a few select people whom you don't know, and you may trade your newly acquired information with people your fellow conspirator doesn't know.

You each have traded information for your own benefit, but you've also participated in building a small network of information traders. You may not know the scope of that network, and you may not even realize you're part of a network at all, but you *are*, and this network constitutes a conspiracy as Assange understands it. No one sat down and agreed to form such a network of inside information traders—the network has simply emerged naturally from local individual bargains. Hence, we can call it an "emergent conspiracy."

Emergent conspiracies like this needn't be restricted to the business world. Suppose I'm a reporter, and I want some hot news to report. A government official offers to give me some inside information, but does so with the understanding that I hold the information for a while (or that I withhold part of it, or "embargo the information" as it's commonly called). I get my scoop, and the government official gets to control the conditions under which the information is made public. I'm now (unknowingly) part of a larger conspiracy. In other words, I'm participating in a conspiracy by respecting the secrets that the network wishes to keep and releasing the secrets (perhaps misinformation) only when it's in the interests of the network to do so. Whether I know or even admit it, I have become a part of that network and hence, a part of the conspiracy.

Here's a third example. Suppose the leader of an Arab country wants the United States to take strong action against Iran. If the Arab leader's people knew he took such a position, there would be strong political blowback and resistance (and possible political risk for him). So, he conducts his discussions with the United States in secret. He has become part of a conspiracy with the United States (and *vice versa*).

In his 2006 essay, "Conspiracy as Governance," Assange described the phenomenon this way: "Plans which assist authoritarian rule, once discovered, induce resistance. Hence these plans are concealed by successful authoritarian powers."

These three illustrations all show the central feature of what Assange takes to be a conspiracy—secrecy and exchange of information within a closed network. Assange believes these closed networks are problematic, but it's important to stress that this is conspiracy in the etymological sense of "conspire": to "breathe with" or "breathe together." In other words, the individuals involved are "of one voice," acting in concert, whether by plan or not, and the secrecy ensures that the benefits of the network accrue to those inside the network (and to the network itself) and not those outside of it.

So, such conspiracies don't involve bald old men sitting around a mahogany table cooking up some plan, nor are they organized on the links of a golf course or in a sauna. Conspiracies can *self-organize* without any conscious effort from anyone. They can be *emergent*.

Are Conspiracies Bad?

So, what's wrong with conspiracies? Problems arise when they become extremely powerful, because whatever the intentions of the individuals within the network, the network itself is optimized for its own success, and not for the benefit of those outside the network. Again, this isn't by design on the part of the conspirators; it's just an emergent property of such systems that they function in this way. People who don't act to benefit their neighboring nodes in the network will eventually be expunged from the system because those neighboring nodes will minimize contact. Those acting in concert with their co-conspirators will form stronger ties and will benefit from the information and financial goods that participation in the network delivers.

Conspirators in the network may *think* they're working for the benefit of others (the individuals in the US military-industrial-congressional complex may well think they're acting for the benefit of the American people, but this is only so much self-deception); they're actually acting for the network.

Even if you're a member of the network, it's not clear that you ultimately benefit except in the obvious ways that you may receive power and wealth. The cost of this Faustian bargain is that you must surrender your creativity. Assange talks about such conspiracies acting against "people's will to truth, love and self-realization," and here I believe he means that members of the conspiracy aren't acting for the love of other individuals or for finding truth outside of the network but rather are acting for the survival of the conspiracy-network itself.

One point that Assange doesn't speak about directly is that conspiracies can also lead to group-think, and thus are threats to self-realization. Two conspirators who routinely exchange lots of information with one another don't merely exchange information but may well develop tight social relationships as a result. So, for example, military contractors and congressmen don't merely exchange information; they also socialize together (at expensive Washington restaurants and on pheasant hunting trips in South Dakota, for example). This creates the possibility of *attitudinal entrainment.*

Entrainment is a term in psychology that refers to the way in which human agents sync up with each other. They might sync up in the way they speak or how they use terms, or for that matter they may sync up in their political attitudes. The point seems obvious enough: people who spend time together start to think in similar ways. The closed network itself becomes a system in which, as attitudes propagate and normalize within the network, network members come to have shared values. In an established network, sharing such values may even be (or become) a prerequisite for entering the network. Because the network is closed, the shared attitudes in the network need not and probably won't be in tune with those outside the network.

So, Assange believes that conspiracies are bad and that they should be dismantled, and this leads to the question of how we go about doing that. Since conspiracies are really just networks of individuals, we need to ask how we can dismantle or damage networks, and this leads us to the question of how networks (in particular, conspiratorial networks) are organized. Before we can attack one, we have to understand how it works.

How Do Conspiracies Work?

Let's start with Assange's own illustration of the way a conspiratorial network functions, from his article "Conspiracy as Governance." Suppose we pound some nails into a wooden board. Let's say that the nails represent the *conspirators*. Now, take some twine and loop it from nail to nail without cutting it. This twine will represent *communication* between the conspirators. So, for example, you might wrap the twine around a nail once and then move on to the next nail and loop the twine again. This would represent a line of communication between the two conspirators. We can continue this way until there's twine connecting all the nails on the board.

You can travel from any nail to any other nail on the board by following the twine. There's a line of communication connecting any two conspirators. And, if they are some distance from each other, then they may be unaware that this line of communication exists between them (they may even be unaware of their own mutual existence). That doesn't matter; they are nonetheless *connected*.

Sometimes co-conspirators don't trust each other. That doesn't matter either, because the information can still flow from one conspirator to another via other paths. Some conspirators are on the "fringe" of the conspiracy, while others are central and communicate with many conspirators. Parts of the board of nails may be densely interconnected with twine. For that matter, there may be several densely interconnected areas with only a narrow bandwidth of communication (few strands of twine) connecting them.

This describes what network theorists would call a "scale-free" network. It's a network with unevenly distributed links, structured somewhat like an airline flight path map with a handful of heavily interconnected hubs (the Internet is such a network, as is the human brain). Such networks are highly resilient because you can't destroy the network by randomly destroying nodes. You would have to target the hubs simultaneously. (More on shutting down the network in a bit.)

Finally, Assange argues that we may also want to model the *importance* of the information flowing between the nodes. In this case, he suggests that we could represent the importance of the information by the *thickness* of the twine connecting the nodes. (Personally, I would have used thickness of the twine to represent the volume of information flow between nodes, perhaps using a color coding system to represent importance.) Ignoring the amount of actual information flow, some channels between nodes (that is, between conspirators) are more important than others. And, what makes a channel of communication important is that it's a channel that tends to carry important information. So, what counts as important information?

Assange says there's no easy answer to this question. It depends entirely on the specific conspiracy. Information that might be of great importance to one conspiracy could be unimportant to another. Thus, information *channels* that might be important to one conspiracy would be unimportant to another. The guiding rule of thumb says the information is more important if it contributes to the well-being and optimal functioning *of the conspiracy itself.* In other words, the only measure of the importance of information (and thus the importance of lines of communication) within a conspiracy is the importance of the information to the health of the conspiracy, which ultimately exists for its own sake.

Clearly, the importance of information and information channels can change over time. Conspiracies are nothing if not dynamic systems. They are, in some respects, *organic* systems. They adapt to their environment as they encounter new sources of information and new obstacles to their survival. Part of this adaptation process involves re-routing information flow within a conspiracy. If a conspirator is exposed as untrustworthy, the conspiracy must re-route the flow of information around that conspirator. Or, if a group of nodes in the conspiracy is destroyed, the conspiracy must again re-route the flow of information within the network. Moreover, channels that carry useless information flow in the beginning may develop into channels that carry critical information as the network evolves and adapts.

Do Conspiracies Think?

Given that their content is information and their form is an adaptive system, Assange thinks of conspiracies as information *processing* systems. As he puts it, a conspiracy is "a type of device that has inputs (information about the environment), a computational network (the conspirators and their links to each other) and outputs (actions intending to change or maintain the environment)." Not only can conspiracies change the environment; they do it better than you or I can. They are "able to outthink the same group of individuals acting alone."

Indeed, because it's a scale-free network, a conspiracy is structured like the organization of neurons in the brain, and the comparison to the brain isn't entirely meta-phorical. Conspiracies are "cognitive devices," according to Assange. They're actually *thinking* systems. They have plans. They have goals. They have needs. They represent states of the world. Often, they have desires about how others should view the world. They routinely want others to form false beliefs about the world. They certainly want to change the world.

This doesn't mean, though, that conspiracies are *conscious*. There's some distance between a "thinking" system that has plans and goals and a system that's also conscious. It is, however, a cognitive system in the sense that it can represent the world, and it can compute strategies and then act on them. If you get in its way, it can mess you up.

So far, we've worked through Assange's arguments that conspiracies are bad and that they should be dismantled, and we've also seen that they're cognitive systems, organized (like the brain) as scale-free networks with plans and intentions, as well as the ability to process information about the environment and even the ability to deceive us. So how do we get rid of them?

Dismantling Conspiracies

One error would be to think that conspiracies can be dismantled by eliminating their leaders, just as the United States government seems obsessed with targeting heads of terrorist networks, drug cartels, and indeed targeting Assange himself as the head of the WikiLeaks network. But, the genius insight of Assange here is that these conspiracies *don't have heads*. It's pointless to try to target a single leader, or even a handful of leaders. The conspiracy is a distributed network, and it most likely can't be taken down by neutralizing key players.

Imagine that our wooden board has one hundred nails all connected by a single length of twine wrapped around the nails. How many nails would you have to pull out before the network of twine fell apart? 10? 20? 50? Assange thinks that this isn't the way to target the network. Instead, we intercept the information flow in the network.

There are two ways this might play out. One possibility is that once the information is leaked, it's no longer closely held and is therefore no longer valuable, no longer a source of power for the network. In some cases, the network may detect the source of the leak and act to plug the hole. In this case, the network undergoes a kind of fission, by severing the link to the leaky node and partially if not completely separating itself from that part of the network where the leak occurred.

This is what Assange proposes in his essay "State and Terrorist Conspiracies": "How can we reduce the ability of a conspiracy to act? . . . We can split the conspiracy, reducing or eliminating important communication between a few high weight links or many low weight links." Thus, even if the network survives, it may well be forced to split into parts. In this case, the network becomes less powerful, even though it still exists and is still a conspiracy. It's simply a weaker conspiracy (or weaker conspiracies).

In addition to the weakening effect of fission, there's a second consequence of leaks. Leaks place a *cognitive tax* on the network. If the conspirators can't trust each other with their information, then they are less likely to exchange it, and this adds a cognitive expense to the information processing that the network undertakes.

Assange's way of putting this is that a culture of leaking places a "secrecy tax" on conspiracies. It makes them paranoid, and this leads to establishing stricter protocols for internal communications. It makes the conspiracy less efficient. Of course, benevolent organizations are affected as well, but the secrecy tax affects them less.

This is how Assange explains the difference, in a 2006 blog post with the unforgiving title "The Nonlinear Effects of Leaks on Unjust Systems of Governance": "In a world where leaking is easy, secretive or unjust systems are nonlinearly hit relative to open, just systems." In other words, good organizations are affected less than bad ones. Why? Because unjust systems, by their nature, create opposition, and in many places the systems "barely have the upper hand." As a result, mass leaking leaves them "exquisitely vulnerable to those who seek to replace them with more open forms of governance." In other words, leaking becomes a kind of chemotherapy that is able to kill off the bad conspiracies while not hurting the good part of the body politic. The net result for malicious conspiracies is a "system-wide cognitive decline" that makes it harder for the conspiracy to stay powerful.

Philosophy Again

Assange's thoughts on conspiracies and how to attack them can be thought of as good examples of how philosophy ought to proceed. Before the nineteenth century, the distinction between philosophy and science wasn't recognized. "Natural philosophy" was a thing, and thinkers from Descartes to Newton self-identified as natural philosophers in the sense that they didn't distinguish between their philosophical and scientific projects.

This unified view of science and philosophy runs through the history of philosophy beginning with Thales (who's often credited with being the first Western philosopher) and continuing through Aristotle, the Middle Ages, and into the modern era. Sometimes the contemporary academy also makes a distinction between practical philosophy and theoretical philosophy, but this distinction too, is artificial. Before the nineteenth century, philosophers wouldn't have recognized this distinction any more than they would have recognized a distinction between science and philosophy.

Assange's work on conspiracy is a paradigmatic example of philosophy in precisely this sense. It connects with some of the new sciences of our day (for example network theory and the theory of emergent systems), helps us to understand how they work, applies them to an understanding of the political, corporate, and social institutions of our world, provides a diagnosis of how those institutions go bad, and finally provides us with strategies for degrading and replacing those corrupt institutions.

Science, theory, and practice are three aspects of a single, unified project. In this particular case, the project is to identify, understand, and dismantle the network-based conspiracies of our world.

2
Leaks in the Ship of Fools

ROBERT F.J. SEDDON

Moral philosophy explores the most fundamental nature of the right and the good, the dutiful, the virtuous, and other such fine and worthy concepts. "Sauce for the gander" is neither fine nor worthy, and so it would be a rare course in ethics that included seminars on the world's smallest violin, or lectures on how to enjoy the sight of chickens coming home to roost. No one ever received a certificate for noticing "One rule for them and another for us" or cases of "Do as I say, not as I do."

The NSA dislikes losing control of its secrets when its secret activities include spying on allied nations' governments? Who would have thought it! Hillary Clinton's presidential candidacy suffered from leaked e-mails, after Clinton took such care with e-mail secrecy when Secretary of State that her use of a private server for official communications created a scandal? Handkerchiefs at the ready! Julian Assange has been pursued by the Swedish state, the same Swedish state that leaked details of every vehicle owner in the country to unvetted workers outside of Sweden when it outsourced work to IBM? People who find the charge of rape against him plausible might still rather sit on their hands than clap and cheer.

A philosopher who's done both kinds of teaching once stated that ethics courses in philosophy departments aim at moral *sophistication*, at producing graduates who can reason through the nuances when some new moral dilemma arises; by contrast, ethics courses in business schools aim to inculcate moral *sensitivity*, to get people to consider ethics in the first place when they have a chance to dip their hands in the till. Yes, those bangs and splashes you can hear involve fish in a barrel, but in the age of WikiLeaks we know plenty about how grubby the world is despite all those efforts to cultivate both sensitivity and sophistication.

WikiLeaks exposes a moral problem—but it's not the kind of problem that could neatly appear in an ethics course at a university. ("The world isn't just sickeningly corrupt; it's flagrantly hypocritical about it. Discuss.") This is a very convenient situation for the status quo, given how many alumni of elite universities have done something leak-worthy. Fortunately, even if it's written by academics this volume isn't a textbook, and philosophy has always had its less staid and prim and pompous side. Diogenes the Cynic (412–323 B.C.E.) is supposed to have wandered about with a lantern in broad daylight— searching for an honest man. (And you wondered why we call it *cynicism*?) Now we have WikiLeaks to shine a light into some murky places, and it shows us just how far (or not) the human condition has progressed.

Becoming Rational

Philosophers traditionally understand the pleasure of watching the high and mighty get taken down a peg or two. No comprehensive course in Western philosophy would be complete without a taste of Plato's dialogues, in which his mentor Socrates (around 470–399 B.C.E.) pesters the great and good of ancient Athens with posers about the nature of piety and justice and all the other high principles they claim to espouse. In this tradition, Socrates is the gadfly whose sting jerks people awake. The same may be said today of WikiLeaks.

Some of Socrates's fellow citizens seem to have thought he was more the kind of jerk who kicks over other people's sandcastles. Being lampooned by the comic playwright Aristophanes didn't shut him up. Being executed did, but Plato's dramatizations created a posthumous Socrates who increasingly turned from a pesky gadfly into a sage with grand designs. Plato's own designs were based on the ruler of Syracuse: reportedly Plato hoped to educate him as a philosopher-king but got himself imprisoned instead. His most accomplished pupil, Aristotle, went on to tutor Alexander the Great.

From convicted gadfly to imperial insider and establishment figure in three generations: selling out or survivalism, depending on your interpretation. (Plato was a contemporary of Diogenes. They didn't entirely get on.) Concerns about philosophy's proper relation to worldly power, or at least an academic payroll and the contortions involved in wringing grant money from funding bodies, continue to this day. Philosophers' sharpest critics are usually other philosophers, keeping the gadfly spirit alive.

Analytic philosophy is the predominant kind in modern English-speaking academia: it champions the kind of clarity and logical rigor with which a mathematician would feel at home. If you look to philosophy for visionary imaginings of alternative societies, a lot of analytic philosophy is going to disappoint you—though for the same reason that nobody looks to mathematicians for radical social criticism. ("So what does higher order type theory say about *racial* types, then?") Analytic philosophy is usually contrasted with Continental philosophy. The stereotypical

Continental philosopher can find histories of injustice in a restaurant menu, ideology in the way you tie your shoelaces, and the prospect of rapturous pleasure in a French art house film festival.

That doesn't mean any kind of philosophy is a passive or complicit tool of the establishment. Bertrand Russell (1872–1970), one of the Analytic tradition's founding figures, was once imprisoned for anti-war activism. No, the Socratic legacy is subtler than that. The actual charges against Socrates involved corrupting the youth and failing to recognize the gods; the Socrates portrayed by Plato thinks the real danger to youthful ears comes from Homer and other poets who portrayed the gods as a bunch of squabbling sitcom characters. The gods of Athens (plural) were a polytheistic pantheon. Plato's Socrates enquires into the nature of the good (singular).

A pantheon like the Greek one may have a king, but it has no *rational* ordering: there's no logical precedence between, say, a god of war and a goddess of love. There may even be a trickster figure, like Hermes for the Greeks or Loki among the Norse gods, who ensures that even divinities can be hurt and humiliated for laughs. Start with such a view of the world, and WikiLeaks will fit snugly into it. The trickster may not be kind, or friendly, or even safe to be around—but when your existence involves dependence on powerful forces over which you can exert little influence, seeing one power pull down another's trousers is *hilarious* and not a little gratifying.

Despite his legacy as philosophy's own trickster, Socrates also belongs to the tradition that eclipsed such views of things. A taste of them lingers in Plato because he wrote dialogues, cleverer dramas than the dramatists', subtler lampooning than Aristophanes's, look, no hands. (Aristophanes appears as a character in Plato's *Symposium* just to underline the point.) Instead of dialogues, Aristotle's surviving work consists of treatises or lecture notes. The old Greek fascination with struggle and contests between competitors was giving way to drier scholarship. The scholars of mediaeval Christian monotheism then put Aristotle on a pedestal, where he remained largely undisturbed until the Renaissance.

Becoming Reasonable

Reason is not cozy, as people learn if they get laid off during corporate "rationalization." Unreason may have led to lynch mobs, but reason produces organization men, and leakers, whistleblowers are treated as renegades not merely because they disturb the rich and powerful, but because they threaten the efficient running of the system.

There's an infamous remark from the Nineties, by a co-founder of the IT company Sun Microsystems: "You have zero privacy anyway. Get over it." (Sun was later acquired by a company called Oracle. Antitrust concerns in Europe were dropped following an American diplomatic intervention which was later revealed by WikiLeaks.) In 2017, asked about Julian Assange's plans to give tech companies access to hacking tools leaked from the CIA, his most optimistic thought was that at least companies don't enjoy the monopoly powers of government.

Christian monotheism had already got over it centuries before, but Christianity looks forward to the judgment of a single perfect God. As the Renaissance gave way to the Enlightenment with the development of science, the Lord who made all, sees all, and knows all seeped into the thoughts of philosophers as a guarantor of the rational ordering of the universe that makes science possible. For René Descartes (1596–1650), God was more clearly and certainly knowable by reason than His physical world is to our senses. George Berkeley (1685–

1753) thought that, in reality, there's no world that exists independently of minds thinking about it, but in his philosophy God is the supreme thinker that holds it all together.

Ideas like those have widely lost their luster, for Christian philosophers nearly as much as for atheists, but the conviction that we live in a fundamentally rational, coherent universe remains strong. We have the successes of the natural sciences to support it. We know the universe of mathematical physics and chemistry is a rational place.

Political philosophy has never had quite that same level of sublime confidence in a sane and sense-making universe, because political philosophers have kept noticing that we live in a world of squabbling states and jostling rivals. And yet, the great questions have been about the one true *template* for the state: during the Cold War, the clash of ideas was between democratic capitalism and Soviet communism. Then Soviet communism went the way of most grand theories and collapsed in practice. Chinese communism survives in practice by being capitalist. North Korea is North Korea.

Once the heady glee of victory had worn off (and the freshly mercantile Chinese started flexing their economic muscles), we had time to look soberly around at what kind of victory we had achieved.

Becoming Cynical

The highest achievement of our rational, scientific, technological civilization is the computer, a machine of perfect logic and tireless calculation. The greatest accomplishment of computing is the Internet, a global network for communication and sharing knowledge. And the most ruthlessly rational things on the Internet are all the advertising networks that track your every movement from site to site in pursuit of economic gain, allowing you, the consumer, to enjoy the benefits of having your details bought and sold. There's a coldly rational universe, all right, but it's hard to glimpse a grand design in it—not because more of us now doubt the existence of our Lord in Heaven, but because seeing and knowing and judging all we do no longer strikes us as holy.

The technology press, which once promised the sleek future of an "information superhighway," now brings to mind a guidebook on ways to die in rural Australia. Are shops tracking your smartphone? Is your "smart" thermostat spying on you? Are your children's voice-activated toys transmitting their conversations to a foreign server? Will your Roomba start selling floor plans of your house to interested third parties?

Scholarly work is no more cheering: in the future keenly anticipated by a report of the UK's Higher Education Commission, students will have their library visits tracked, their *eyeballs* tracked when reading electronic textbooks, and even their visits to the campus bar tracked, all in order to accumulate data "which can be used in analytics to provide a more complete and powerful portrait of the student." If there's any doubt, just consider the controversy surrounding Cambridge Analytica's use of data mining in the 2016 US presidential election.

In this world, leakage of personal data isn't an aberration. In this world, WikiLeaks is far from being the most disturbing thing. It plausibly contributes to the public good, unlike, for example, poorly secured baby monitors that have allowed voyeuristic strangers to intercept the video stream. Denizens of a world in which there's a site called haveibeenpwned.com (just so you can find out who failed to keep your data secure when public breaches occur) might reasonably wonder whether there's really anything that special about WikiLeaks—apart, of course, from its penchant for getting up the noses of powerful organizations.

At least philosophers didn't invent this state of affairs. When Karl H. Marx (1818–1883) decided that philosophy should go beyond simply describing the world and actually try to change it, and that he had sussed out how the inherent contradictions of capitalism would *necessarily* resolve themselves through a process culminating in violent revolution, he gave intellectual impetus to what turned out to be a whole series of totalitarian disasters.

Communist dictatorships came to embody uniform rationality by imposing centralized control and surveillance upon entire populations. This secured Marx's place in the canonical list of Great Philosophers, but there he gets to rub shoulders with Martin Heidegger (1889–1976), who for a time supported the National Socialist Party.

We capitalist nations have ended up with mass surveillance, too, but at least we get to blame merely greed-obsessed profit-seeking advertisers for it . . . along with social networking sites, credit card processors, government agencies, and numerous other parties before we even start thinking about political philosophers.

While the state of the world may not be the way any philosopher planned it, we still get the task of working out how to do philosophy that grapples with it. When you're disposed to expect a cogent, rational universe, you'll more easily conceive of emperors (clothes or no) than of bickering tribes or rival robber barons. You'll be better prepared for the dystopia of Orwell's Big Brother than to see privacy die the death of a thousand cuts as a script on a web page auctions off your eyeballs. And yet, it's the latter we encounter as human beings living in the modern world.

So there's a certain self-critical unease about the tradition that leads down to us from Plato's Academy (yes, he founded the first institution to be called an academy), the kind that might make you tempted to grab a lamp and go about like Diogenes the Cynic (you see what I mean now). It's not a concern of the usual sort philosophers have, about incoherent ideas or fallacious arguments. It's the awkward shuffling of feet when you hear how many of the British governing class passed through the Philosophy, Politics, and Economics course at Oxford, and you realize that this is what it's like to have become part of the increasingly malfunctioning machine. It's a bit hard to blame the whole malaise on the economists and the political scientists.

Becoming Bemused

Twenty-four centuries after Socrates, we've rediscovered that we live in Homer's universe, the poet's paradise: the gods are plural, and they squabble, and they vie for sordid power. The Greek gods' messenger was Hermes, who was also the trickster and transgressor, god of thieves and inventor of lies. And we in turn have learnt much about so many modern notables from WikiLeaks, which naturally swims in the same muddy waters as those it exposes. Insinuating questions about whose backing WikiLeaks might enjoy, with eyebrows waggled in the direction of Russia, are of limited effect against a trickster god.

We mortals, the little people who've been told time and again that we have nothing to fear if we've nothing to hide, can hardly miss the irony: a dark and double irony when WikiLeaks itself wields murky influence on our politics.

Socrates might have appreciated the joke: he was the master ironist, the gadfly who knew that the most simple and artless and naïve of questions are the best for exposing the pretensions of the high and mighty. In the early dialogues, before he turns into a mouthpiece for Plato, discussion may lead down the garden path and peter out in unresolved perplexity. And maybe there is no ultimate Truth about WikiLeaks, or none we'd have a clue what to do with if we had it.

Plato may have vied for victory over Aristophanes and the dramatists, but he studied his rivals closely enough to have a vivid sense of the tragicomedy of human life. One of the images he's left us is that of the ship of fools, with a crew of mutinous and quarrelling sailors. In the struggle for control the advantage goes to the most persuasive flatterers, not the unworldly 'stargazers' who actually know how to navigate by the constellations. This is supposed to soften you up to accept enlightened despotism: seeing the Athenian democracy kill Socrates persuaded Plato that ruling is a skill and a career for experts, and what every state really needed was a benevolent dictator, preferably one educated by Plato.

Something about this farce may seem dramatically familiar.

If my grand conclusion had been that philosophy can tell you you're surrounded by fools, you might, I concede, feel a little short-changed. Still, the Fool (capitalized with cap and bells) is a notoriously ambiguous figure, being at once both idiot and jester, innocent simpleton and speaker of truth to power.

Friedrich Nietzsche (1844–1900), one of the most tragicomic of philosophers, called Socrates a buffoon who got himself taken seriously. So the noblest, most sagacious icon of our logic-chopping discipline is . . . a clown. Søren Kierkegaard (1813–1855), who wrote his doctoral dissertation on Socrates and irony, imagined a clown coming on stage to warn the audience that a fire has broken out: they think it's part of his act and laugh and clap.

Ludwig Wittgenstein (1889–1951), an austere philosopher of logic and language, examined scenarios that may have been inspired by slapstick and *commedia dell'arte*. The Renaissance humanist Desiderus Erasmus (1466–1536) wrote a satire called *In Praise of Folly*, in which Folly, personified, delivers a lecture in praise of herself.

Perhaps we need clowns; perhaps we need tricksters. The age of science and reason has given us technocrats who turn out, now that the ship of fools has sprung so many leaks, to have the exact same moral failings that have been part of the human condition always and everywhere. It's the grubby side of human life that creates a need for WikiLeaks, as it has for private eyes, investigative journalists—and moral philosophers.

The age of science and reason doesn't know how to deal with this. Technology is ridiculous: with the greatest communications network of all time at our fingertips, we find we've progressed to being easier targets for mass surveillance than ever before.

Politics is ridiculous: democratic state bureaucracies accumulate data about their citizens in hope of working out what these strange, unruly beings are actually thinking.

And philosophy is ridiculous: philosopher John Cottingham observes that philosophers now get asked about their "research methods" as though they were scientists, and giving an honest answer—"reading some books and thinking about some ideas"—is not a career-enhancing move.

WikiLeaks demonstrates that our elites are as grubbily ridiculous as everybody else: even the ones who don't prove it themselves on social media. In its way, it humanizes them.

Second Dump

Deep Thoughts

3
Blind Oversight

TRIP MCCROSSIN AND AZEEM CHAUDRY

The "United States Intelligence Community" is a collection of seventeen separate government agencies that work both independently and in concert conducting intelligence activities to support United States foreign policy and national security.

Established by President Ronald Reagan in December of 1981, it was to be governed by the National Security Act of 1947. The earliest version of the entry, "United States Intelligence Community," in the online open-source encyclopedia Wikipedia was posted in March of 2004, a few short months into the 108th Congress, during which the Intelligence Reform and Terrorism Prevention Act was proposed, debated, and ultimately adopted, significantly amending the National Security Act in response to the *9/11 Commission Report*. The timing is made more interesting still by a related observation.

On the one hand, while the Wikipedia entry has since grown six-fold, and includes much that's of general interest, it includes no section dedicated to "Controversy" or the like, though at least it does include an external link to the *Washington Post*'s Top Secret America investigation. The entry dedicated to the 2004 Act doesn't include even that much. On the other hand, the entry devoted to WikiLeaks, from which we have learned so much that's at best unflattering about the Intelligence Community, does have such a section dedicated to controversy, and it's roughly one-third of the entry's content.

This observation isn't meant to suggest that WikiLeaks doesn't deserve criticism, but rather that its actions have made the Intelligence Community at least as notably controversial, and yet there's no corresponding section that deals with that controversy. To acknowledge this is to be better able, in turn, to defend WikiLeaks against at least part of the most philosophically substantial of the criticisms against it, those regarding the moral hazard entailed by its actions. The following is designed to explore such a defense.

One Person's Moral Hazard . . .

The authors of the *9/11 Commission Report* admitted, shockingly, that "few members of Congress have the broad knowledge of intelligence activities or the know-how about technologies employed." In response, the Kennedy Center produced for them a briefing book in 2009 with the provocative title, *Confrontation or Collaboration? Congress and the Intelligence Community*. In it, the authors acknowledge that the Intelligence Community's size and complexity "often confuse and stymie lawmakers attempting to understand intelligence issues," while admitting that "new and unforeseen challenges will certainly arise" during their tenure, offering the ideas presented in the briefing as a general framework on many of the issues they will undoubtedly encounter. One of these challenges, as it would turn out only a year later, was the rise of WikiLeaks in the public's consciousness.

Intelligence, in broad terms, entails the "collection, analysis, and production of sensitive information to support national security leaders, including policymakers, military commanders, and Members of Congress." It also seeks to safeguard these processes and information by means of counterintelligence activities that "stymie the efforts of foreign intelligence services and manipulate information to confuse foreign intelligence gathering."

To all intents and purposes, then, the Intelligence Community functions as a non-canonical branch of the US Armed Forces, designed to provide tactical advantage to the other, canonical, five branches (Army, Navy, Air Force, Marines, and Coast Guard). Its weapon of choice is an ever-expanding array of electronic surveillance techniques, subject, just like the techniques of the Armed Forces, to Congressional oversight.

Oversight in the case of the canonical five is meant to ensure, at least in principle, observance of certain rules of engagement as laid out by an advocate of just war theory. These rules are primarily four:

First, military engagement should discriminate between combatants and non-combatants, harming as few non-combatants as possible.

Second, it should be tactically proportional in securing its military objective.

Third, it should abjure weapons that are "evil in themselves," such as nuclear, chemical, or biological weapons, or tactics that are terroristic.

Finally, it should entail no sacrifice of civil liberties "at home," the safeguarding of which is, after all, at least ostensibly, the point of warfare in the first place.

Shouldn't the Intelligence Community, as a non-canonical branch, be held just as accountable?

WikiLeaks grounds itself in the core conviction that indeed it *should* be, and it's motivated by evidence that the Intelligence Community is *not* being held properly accountable. What it has revealed is, generally speaking, two-fold.

On the one hand, the Intelligence Community routinely engages in an additional form of counterintelligence devoted to obscuring most of its gathered intel from public view. On the other hand, it's motivated to do so, at least in part, by the nature of these activities, which all too often reflect violations of the aforementioned rules of engagement that are at best unsavory, at worst unethical—WikiLeaks's *Collateral Murder*, *Afghan War Diary,* and *Iraq War Logs* revelations, all released in 2010, or those released the following year regarding the treatment of detainees at the Guantanamo Bay Detention Center, are all examples.

But Two Wrongs . . .

The manner of its two-fold general revelation, however, has rendered WikiLeaks vulnerable to a familiar sort of critique, which is that its individual revelations, depending on just how they're made, may be morally hazardous.

A moral hazard occurs when an individual or organization is willing to increase their exposure to risk because they're insulated from the moral effects—responsibility, blameworthiness, accountability—of their risky business, especially when another individual or organization will bear the costs of those risks.

In the above four cases, if either sources and methods generally, or intelligence operatives or civilians specifically, are knowingly revealed in the process, this risks compromising, also knowingly, the specific individuals' or the public's safety in general.

In the case of WikiLeaks's release of material in which the names of Afghan civilians hadn't been redacted, the result was a joint rebuke, issued by Amnesty International, the Open Society Institute, the Campaign for Innocent Victims in Conflict, and the Afghanistan Independent Human Rights Commission, for putting these otherwise innocent people in jeopardy.

But, even if it isn't the case that sources and methods, or operatives or civilians, are revealed, what if government officials or parties to its political process are nonetheless embarrassed, as in the 2010 diplomatic cables and the 2016 Democratic National Committee email revelations? In this case, the government or governments in question may become less effective as a result, which may again compromise public safety.

In the extreme, such behavior may be morally damnable, as Sue Halpern implies in her *New York Review of Books* article, "The Nihilism of Julian Assange." Assange, and by implication WikiLeaks, she contends has no interest in anyone's privacy but their own and their sources', acting as though private communications and personal information are "fair game," calling it a "nihilism" that elevates freedom "to a principle that gives him license to act without regard to consequences."

As Halpern is no doubt aware, nihilism, used without further qualification, picks out a variety of perspectives. What she must mean here, in particular, is either *moral* or *political* nihilism. In the former case, however, she'd be asserting that Assange denies, generally speaking, the coherence of moral language, or at least the moral language conventionally in play in our era, and so finds the moral hazard critique without merit.

This would seem inconsistent, however, with how Assange describes himself in his exchange, in *Risk*, with Lady Gaga. "Let's not pretend I'm a normal person," he muses, seeing as he's "obsessed with political struggle," where the struggle can't help but be defined by WikiLeaks's revelations as resisting *injustice*. This suggests that Assange's and WikiLeaks's nihilism is of a more *political* sort.

Needless to say, there's a certain irony in Assange opening himself and WikiLeaks up to being described as politically nihilistic, given political nihilism's roots in the nineteenth-century opposition to Russian Tsarism and the recent allegations that Assange and WikiLeaks were complicit in Russia's meddling in the 2016 US presidential elections. However, precisely because he's *not* a moral nihilist and believes that governmental structures have in many ways failed us in moral terms, he's prepared to deny, generally speaking, the coherence of government, or at least the government conventionally in play in our era.

WikiLeaks responds to the moral hazard critique in this spirit, that is, by asserting that what's ultimately at issue is *whistle-blowing*—a measure of last resort in exposing injustice, when the *rule of law* is unavailable or insufficiently helpful in addressing it.

In effect, WikiLeaks despairs of anything short of its style of whistle-blowing being able, given current circumstances, to pry loose intelligence that the public has a vested interest in knowing, even a *right* to know. How else may we judge, after all, whether and to what degree we're prepared to suffer "dirty hands" by being complicit in unsavory or unethical rules-of-engagement violations committed on behalf of the public's interest in knowing or their right to know? The strategy isn't to deny its own moral hazard, but to mitigate or even justify it as a *response* to the prior moral hazard of the Intelligence Community. In other words, it's an attempt to justify exposing unjust, or at least morally questionable, activities that are kept secret, hidden from public scrutiny.

As such, it appears to be an instance of a familiar distinction between what we *intend* and what we *foresee*, which goes something like this. We, WikiLeaks, *intend* to reveal injustice—the alleged murders revealed in the *Collateral Murder* footage, say. We also *foresee* that, as an *un*intended consequence of what we intend, harm may result—suffered by the alleged *Collateral Murder* murderers, say, or worse, by others closely or loosely associated with them. As long as the former benefit outweighs the latter harm, however, *in some meaningful sense*, then the latter doesn't undermine the alleged justice of the former. But, the assertion that there's some such "meaningful sense" is frequently decried as establishing an untenable *moral equivalence* (the denial that a genuine moral comparison can be made between two competing sides)—untenable because WikiLeaks's whistle-blowing may not be a measure of last resort as the institution appears to want to claim. Isn't there *already* a way to avoid injustice, a WikiLeaks skeptic might ask, short of whistle-blowing? Isn't this what Congressional oversight is meant to accomplish? (See Chapter 4 in this volume for a more detailed account of the doctrine of double effect.)

[Over]see, Said the Blind Man

The Intelligence Reform and Terrorism Prevention Act was defined by Congress as reforming the intelligence community, intelligence, and intelligence-related activities of the United States government in response to perceived intelligence failures in the run-up to September 11th 2001.

Among its principal reforms was the creation of a new position, Director of National Intelligence (DNI). As Erwin and Pelasco put it, this position is designed to "establish priorities and to tailor the intelligence budgets to meet those priorities." The Director oversees the process of developing the overall intelligence budget based on a National Intelligence Priorities Framework that "identifies topics relevant to policymakers and assigns priorities to intelligence targets based on those topics," which, once developed, is submitted to the President for submission ultimately to Congress. Once Congress takes possession of it, the second and third parts of the process kick in, which are Congressional authorization and the appropriation of funds.

The overall process is complex, one might even say baroque, but includes nonetheless an ostensibly straightforward form of oversight, which occurs at the last stage here, the appropriations stage, which is the "power of the purse." What persists, nonetheless, is a problematic tension between intelligence and oversight, arising out of the difficult business of balancing accountability and security given the degree of secrecy ostensibly required. The common sense but oddly challenging assumption is that access to what's to be overseen is key to effective oversight. "Secrecy," however, according to *The 9/11 Commission Report*, "while necessary, can also harm oversight." It continues:

> The overall budget of the intelligence community is classified, as are most of its activities. Thus, the Intelligence committees cannot take advantage of democracy's best oversight mechanism: public disclosure. This makes them significantly different from other congressional oversight committees, which are often spurred into action by the work of investigative journalists and watchdog organizations.

However, almost a decade after the appearance of the 9/11 report, the adoption of *The Intelligence Reform and Terrorism Prevention Act*, and several years after WikiLeaks's 2010 revelations, Elaine Halchin and Frederick Kaiser, writing for the Congressional Research Service, reported that little had changed:

The most significant constraint is the high degree and pervasive-
ness of secrecy surrounding intelligence policy, information,
activities, operations, resources, and personnel. For Congress,
this means that the legislature, its committees, and its Members
are circumscribed in a number of ways: what they know; who
receives the information, how, and in what form and forum; who
provides it; what information can be shared with other Members
and panels, how, and in what detail; and what non-governmental
sources can contribute to legislators' knowledge, to what degree,
and in what ways. The secrecy imperative results in a system
that is often closed to outsiders—not just the general public but
also Representatives and Senators who do not have seats on
the select committees on intelligence.

There's little reason to believe that much, if anything, has
changed since. But how is this state of affairs not, for all
intents and purposes, like saying to someone, "I want you
to let me be up to something, and I also want you to pay
the bill when it comes due, and I wouldn't mind you making
sure that I'm doing the right thing in the process, or at least
not the wrong thing, but I'm sorry, I'm afraid I can't tell you
what I'm planning to be up to"? And how has the situation
not become even more tragically nonsensical in the wake
of what we know from WikiLeaks' revelations?

Secrets and Harms

What Halchin and Kaiser report is surely not in the spirit
of the above passage from the *9/11 Commission Report*.
Assuming the Commission is embracing oversight, that is,
generally speaking, as the above passage would suggest,
and so bemoaning harm done to it, isn't the spirit of that
passage better captured by amending it in something like
the following way: "Secrecy, while [some may be] necessary,
[too much] can also harm oversight."

And in this spirit, might we also want to amend what follows this, in the original, in something like the following way: "The overall budget of the intelligence community is [*now*] classified, as are most of its activities. Thus, the Intelligence committees cannot [*now*] take advantage of democracy's best oversight mechanism: public disclosure. This makes [*these committees, in their current incarnation, unfortunately*] significantly different from other congressional oversight committees, which are often spurred into action by the work of investigative journalists and watchdog organizations."

And if the report had been written ten or more years later, we can also imagine that the last sentence might be amended further still, in something like the following way: "This makes [the Intelligence committees, *in their current incarnation, unfortunately*] significantly different from other congressional oversight committees, which are often spurred into action by the work of investigative journalists and watchdog organizations [*such as, think what we will of them, WikiLeaks's public disclosures*]."

The possibility that's envisioned here isn't unlike what National Security Archive Director Thomas Blanton advocates, in his contribution to a National Public Radio segment on the 2010 diplomatic cables revelation entitled, "Is WikiLeaks Release Brave or Unethical?" "I end up someplace," he admits, "pretty mixed." It's his job, after all, revealing a kind of professional sympathy with WikiLeaks, to try to get such documents loose. And practically, he bemoans, "for twenty-five years, we've been trying to get documents like this out of the government using the rule-of-law system." He nonetheless concedes, however, reflecting the language from the Commission's report, a "necessary tension" between the government and the core conviction that animates his work, and also WikiLeaks's, albeit less responsibly he believes.

Overall, Blanton insists on the one hand that knowing more about what our government does is a good thing, but on the other hand, government has a right to keep at least some secrets, albeit with an important clarification, in the spirit of the above amendment to the above passage from the *Report*, that they be real secrets the revelation of which would put people in danger. "What I disagree with in terms of the WikiLeaks methodology," he continues, isn't the shared conviction that animates it, but the recklessness of forsaking "a rule-of-law process or making the Freedom of Information Act work, where you have that dialogue with the government, the government gets a chance to censor the stuff that would put anybody at risk."

We don't have to go far to find a US government reaction to WikiLeaks that would suggest that dialogue with the government regarding the publication of WikiLeaks-style revelations isn't in the cards in the near future. This was already true on President Obama's watch, and it's only more so on President Trump's. Even so, unauthorized leaks have only increased in number, as leakers' options have flourished, while trust in government secrecy has declined. The mission Assange originally set out to accomplish, to provide a safe way for whistleblowers to hold power account-able, has only sown the seeds of WikiLeaks's possible future obsolescence. Almost every major newspaper, magazine, and website now has some way for leakers to upload their information, and most are through an anonymous, online, open-source drop box called Secure Drop, which also gives leakers the option of choosing where to upload their information.

Did this come about because of WikiLeaks's hazardous behavior? Likely it did. Will WikiLeaks shutter itself or engage in less hazardous behavior if leakers have less hazardous venues to frequent? Likely one or the other will occur, or both. Will WikiLeaks continue to pursue revelations that are considered hazardous when alternatives are unavailable? Likely it will. Will WikiLeaks continue to defend against charges of moral hazard as political nihilistic whistleblower, intending justice, even while foreseeing possible harm? Likely it will.

Whatever comes about, our era is among other things the WikiLeaks era. What government there is in a post-WikiLeaks era is anyone's guess. If there's still a Congress involved, it's likely to need a new briefing book. It might be called, *Collaboration Through Confrontation—Congress and the Intelligence Community in the Wake of WikiLeaks*.

4
The Double Effect of WikiLeaking

DAN MIORI

WikiLeaks is dedicated to the confidential release of secret information over the Internet, ostensibly for the good purpose of holding corporations and governments accountable by telling the truth.

The classical doctrine of "double effect" is a tool to help determine moral responsibility for damage that occurs incidental to our actions. Using the principle of double effect, let's determine whether Julian Assange is responsible for harm caused by his release of this secret information.

Although there are many people who work on and for WikiLeaks, Julian Assange calls the shots. Therefore, we'll consider the actions of WikiLeaks to be the actions of Julian Assange in order to test the principle of double effect.

Opinions differ on just how responsible Assange is for damage caused by his actions. In the Wikipedia article "Reception of WikiLeaks," a full range of international reaction is described. At one end of the spectrum we have fellow Australian and former Prime Minister Kevin Rudd who stated that "The core responsibility . . . goes to those individuals responsible for that initial unauthorised release," simultaneously suggesting both that Aussies are a tight bunch and that Assange is a functionary with little or no effect on the process. An opposing viewpoint might be that of the US government as embodied by former Secretary of State Hillary Clinton, who's opinion can probably be summed up as, "He's completely responsible and we should *string him up by his fucking balls!*"

In July 2010 Assange used WikiLeaks to release hundreds of thousands of documents, hacked from the US government and concerning the war in Iraq, directly to the Internet. The "data dump" included the names of Iraqi civilians who co-operated with the US government. Assange's staff made no effort to remove information which would identify them, which left those civilians open to reprisals by insurgent groups.

That same July, reporters for the British newspaper *The Guardian*, when previewing the documents that WikiLeaks was about to release, raised their concerns over this with Assange. Their impression, as described in the book *Inside Julian Assange's War on Secrecy: WikiLeaks*, was that Assange understood their worries; he just didn't care.

Finally, when discussing his actions in the 2010 Swedish television documentary *Wiki Rebels*, Assange reluctantly agreed that WikiLeaks had caused injury by releasing secret information, but that any harm caused was unintentional and was outweighed by the benefit of releasing it. This is a tacit appeal to the principle of double effect.

Double, Double, Toil and Trouble

The principle of double effect helps us to examine the risks and benefits associated with actions and decision-making, but it's not an absolute measure of moral responsibility. Some scholars feel that double effect isn't a reasonable measure because it suggests that intentions may be more important than outcomes. The doctrine was first proposed by Thomas Aquinas (1225–1274), a Catholic saint and theologian, in his work *Summa Theologica*. When discussing the idea of one individual killing another in self-defense, he stated:

> Nothing hinders one act from having two effects, only one of which is intended, while the other is beside the intention. Accordingly, the act of self-defense may have two effects: one, the saving of one's life; the other, the slaying of the aggressor.

Aquinas then goes on to flesh out his thoughts a bit, but this revolutionary concept only gets a few paragraphs. It would evolve into its current form over several centuries and be applied to issues as complex as how to wage war and as personal as abortion. I say revolutionary because, long before Aquinas, another Catholic saint, Augustine of Hippo (354–430), wrote that any attempt at self-defense came from "inordinate self-love," which Augustine felt was something any good Christian should avoid. Brings extreme meaning to "turn the other cheek." This view held sway for almost a thousand years in the West, until Aquinas proposed the doctrine of double effect.

Fast forward to the modern era. In his essay *An Historical Analysis of the Principle of Double Effect*, Joseph Mangan offers the following formulation: A person may permissibly perform an action that he foresees will produce a double effect if four conditions are *simultaneously* met:

first, the action itself is good or at least morally indifferent

second, the good effect, but *not* the evil effect, is what's intended

third, the good effect isn't produced *by means of* the evil effect

and fourth, there's a *proportionately grave* reason for

permitting the evil effect.

Other formulations have been offered, some in a different order, some with three conditions instead of four; but, since Mangan has been referenced in almost every discussion of double effect in the last sixty years, we'll stick with his version.

The Murdercycle Gang

Recalling Aquinas's case of self-defense, suppose a tattooed motorcycle gang member attacks you. Fearing for your life, you hit him over the head with your Scooby Doo lunchbox, killing him instantly. Since your intent was to defend yourself and not to kill him, you may not be morally responsible for having committed murder. In fact, it may not be *murder* at all.

Using Mangan's criteria, we can say that the *action*, defending yourself, is good or at least morally neutral. You're aware that your lunch box is capable of being a deadly weapon, causing grave injury, but the *evil* effect, killing someone, isn't your intention; defending yourself is. The *good* effect, incapacitating your attacker and thus preventing your own possible demise, isn't necessarily achieved by the evil effect. After all, he might have lived. Lastly, the reason for permitting the evil effect, your own possible demise, is *proportionally grave*. It's a life for a life! Your fierce blandishment of your vittles is in response to some bad-ass motherfucker running at you, not some skinny six-year-old screaming "If I don't get candy RIGHT NOW I'm going to kill someone!" Since all criteria are met simultaneously, you're off the hook morally . . . possibly not legally, but definitely morally.

The Trolley Problem

This is a now-famous example that can be used to explore the doctrine of double effect. Suppose you're standing in front of a switch near a trolley track, and you see an out-of-control trolley headed your way. Further down the tracks, along each of two branches that extend from the switch, are track workers. If the trolley continues along its current path, several unsuspecting workers will be killed. If you switch the track, only one worker will be killed.

Although it sounds unrealistic, this scenario comes a bit closer to a real-world application in that while we are rarely faced with defending our lives, we're constantly put in situations where our decisions will impact others. In this case, as with so many others, not acting is a choice, so it won't allow you to avoid making a decision. This example more clearly illustrates the idea that by choosing the least crappy of two crappy options, you may not be morally responsible for the damage caused by your decision as long as it prevents worse damage.

Applying our four criteria, we see that the *action*, saving the lives of the several track workers by throwing a switch, is morally good. The *evil* effect, the death of the single track worker, isn't an intended effect. In the language of double effect, we say it's "foreseen but unintended." The *good* effect, saving those many lives, doesn't result necessarily from the *evil* effect of the single track worker's death, but from switching the track. Again, as in the Murdercycle Gang scenario, the single track worker could survive. Finally, the *proportionally grave* reason for risking the near certain death of the single worker is the similar death of the several workers. Because all four conditions are met simultaneously, if you throw the switch, you can comfort yourself with the belief that you aren't *morally* responsible for the gory, horrific, technicolor death of the one worker. Of course, that doesn't mean you won't need therapy.

The Palliative Physician

Another frequently used scenario for testing the doctrine

of double effect comes from the field of medicine called palliative care, which includes the treatment of suffering at the end of life. There are a few reasons for using this one. Mercifully, it requires far less sordid imagery. It involves health-care decision-making, which touches all of us, so this is less a thought experiment and more a well discussed example from reality. And, because it's a real-world example of double effect, it illustrates an existing standard for dealing with unavoidable decisions capable of causing a great deal of harm.

Suppose you're a physician whose patient is terminally ill and experiences near constant suffering as a result of their condition. Morphine can provide relief from such pain, but it can also hasten death. If your intent in administering the morphine is to relieve pain, then it's considered good medicine. If the intent is to end suffering by ending a life, however, even with the exact same dose given the exact same way, then it can arguably be considered *murder*. In places where assisted suicide is legal, there are requirements that must be met to take advantage of the process, but to keep the conversation simple we will assume that no such offer has been made to, or accepted by, the patient. You administer a suitable dosage, and though it relieves the pain, it also ends their life.

Applying the four criteria, we can say that the *action*, giving morphine to relieve pain or other symptoms, is good or at least morally neutral. The intended effect, the *good* effect, is the relief of suffering in the many forms that it can take in someone who is terminally ill. That good effect, relieving suffering, is independent of the *evil* effect, that the patient dies. After all, like the other scenarios, the patient might not die. Finally, the extremity of the suffering caused by an irreversible terminal illness is a *proportionally grave* reason for risking potentially shortening the life of someone whose existence can be measured in hours or days, not years.

Because all four criteria are met simultaneously, the doctrine of double effect would imply that you are not morally responsible for the patient's death. And, this would seem to be true *even if* you were very confident that the patient would die as a result, simply because their death is a foreseen but unintended effect.

The actions of palliative care clinicians are scrutinized by hospitals invested in professional practice and the laws governing it; by family members hip deep in the trauma of losing a loved one; by colleagues who may lean more towards preserving life at any cost (especially when that cost is paid by the guy in the bed and not them); but most especially in the United States, by a nation dedicated to nothing so much as advancing the personal injury lawsuit industry (KA-CHING!).

Why palliative care survives this scrutiny can be found in The World Health Organization's definition of it, which states its goal as: the relief of the suffering of patients and their families through "impeccable assessment and treatment of pain and other problems." Meeting this definition requires a conscientious understanding of both the disease process and medical treatment; no oopsies allowed. Difficult decisions aren't always medical decisions, therefore the impeccable understanding of the actions and outcomes justified under double effect in any field are essential. We intuitively accept this in the health care of ourselves and our loved ones. Actions with a risk for causing harm mustn't be casual; they must be thoughtful above reproach, with all possible controllable factors scrupulously minded. Rushing to act may feel satisfying, but it can also cover many sins.

Journalistic Integrity

Journalism, believe it or not, has ethical standards. Not

everyone is as enthusiastic about concepts like accuracy, objectivity, and public accountability or even just getting into the neighborhood of relevancy and rationality, but every news outlet subscribes to some sort of code of ethics. Organizations that do it well, like *The Wall Street Journal* or *The Guardian*, can have diametrically opposed editorial views but still practice in a highly responsible way.

One fundamental premise of those codes of ethics is a commitment to the limitation of harm which can occur when information not central to the story is released. To that end, media outlets will withhold sensitive information like the names of children, names of crime victims, or information which may needlessly harm someone's reputation.

Journalism involves gathering and analyzing information, putting that information into context in a readable form, and making it available for consumption by the public. Part of Julian Assange's argument to avoid the moral responsibility for harm from his release of confidential information involves the fact that he's not a journalist, and truly by the letter of this or any other definition of journalism, he isn't. The only part of the definition, in fact, that he meets is making the information available to the public. Consider this, however: without making the product available to the public, someone who has all the training and skills of a journalist is simply an assistant manager at Walmart. The part of the definition which gives rise to all that ethical soul searching and hand wringing is the fact that people are going to read it. The point, that this action has consequences, stands.

Ass-Man Outs a Snitch

You're an assistant manager at Walmart posting on *Ass-Man*, an assistant manager web-blog, about the arrest of a dangerous neighborhood criminal caught shoplifting in your store. You include the name of the snitch who ratted him out in your post. You didn't mean to do it, it just slipped (you moron). A few days later, you learn that the snitch has been severely beaten and is in the hospital. Are you morally responsible for his condition?

Applying Mangan's four criteria, we can say that posting on *Ass-man* in order to alert the public to the presence of criminal elements in the local community is morally good. The *evil* effect, snitches getting stitches, isn't intended. The *good* effect, stating the truth and informing the public about a local criminal element, wasn't accomplished by the evil effect, snitch stitchery. So far, so good.

Lastly, the *good* effect of informing the public of miscreants in their midst doesn't seem to present *proportionally grave* reason for permitting the *evil* effect, that Larry from electronics has an interesting new facial feature and is laid up in the hospital. Since the release of information doesn't meet all four criteria simultaneously, you would be morally responsible for the harm that results from its release. Ethicists might feel this scenario lacks complexity, but since it includes the emotional appeal of a horrible disfigurement, it will probably pass muster.

The Assange Effect

Putting it all together, let's go back to the 2010 Iraq War data dump by Assange and WikiLeaks. Is the *action* good or at least indifferent? The action is making previously secret information available on the Internet in order to expose morally objectionable practices by those in positions of power. This certainly seems to fit the notion of a good action insofar as any action that reveals immoral or unjust activity is, in that respect, a good thing. Is the *good* effect and not the *evil* effect what is intended?

There's absolutely no evidence that the intent behind

releasing this information was to cause any harm other than to the US government's ability to operate in the shadows. So, Assange meets the second criterion. Is the *good* effect necessarily produced by means of the *evil* effect? No. Exposing morally objectionable military activities, and thus holding the US government accountable, isn't brought about by harm to Iraqi civilians, so he meets the third criterion. Finally, is there a *proportionally grave* reason for permitting the evil effect? The good effect, exposing morally objection- able activities and holding the US accountable for its actions, is at best an existential benefit. It feels good, but was it proportional to an undocumented gruesome end for those Iraqis exposed in the great 2010 data dump? Intuitively, it would seem that to be proportional it would have to have directly saved a shit-ton of lives. It looks more like the benefit in this case amounts to Assange pointing at the US government and yelling "I got you . . . I got you gooood!" An ego boost for Assange, not much comfort for the Wiki ass-fucked.

At best Assange's score at this point is three out of four, but recalling Mangan's assertion, that all four criteria must be met simultaneously, by the principle of double effect he's morally responsible for any damage caused by his 2010 data dump and by any other similarly unfiltered information he has released.

As If!

Having created an argument that holds Assange responsible for harm which arises from how he released information, can there be an argument supporting him? At the somewhat looser end of double effect is the belief that the actions of a superior individual shouldn't be questioned by lesser beings. The argument used to support this is called Bracton's Maxim. Proposed by British jurist Henry De Bracton (1210–1268), it states "that which is otherwise not lawful is made lawful by necessity."

As you might expect, this is a favorite tool of dictators looking to justify actions like shooting peaceful protestors, annexing territory, genocide, stuff like that. Bracton's Maxim is generally interpreted to mean that sometimes, usually under great stress from an outside force, a leader must act in ways that aren't consistent with the letter of the law.

Someone channeling Bracton would get the most traction from the fourth of double effect's criteria, that the *good effect* would be so fantastic that it would be proportional to *any evil effect* of the actions taken. Bracton intended his words to justify decisions by a head of state in a dire national emergency. He also understood that his words would be open to misuse and pointed out that, while a king's will does have the force of law, it must be exercised in accordance with the laws as established by the people whom that regent is responsible to. To quote Bracton; "Under no man, but under God and the law."

Not So Fast

Consider the example of the Palliative Physician again. What if that clinician, at some point in her otherwise scrupulous care of the terminally ill patient, hopes that patient will die? What if that clinician orders a morphine dose increase with the overall intent of treating pain but also understands that it will be the last dose needed? To truly determine intent would involve some next-level telepathy shit. Even if that were possible, we can ask whether good intention is an excuse for allowing (or causing) something bad to happen. Double effect is only a tool, which allows us to examine decision making and come to a better understanding of the morality specific to the situation.

This author's opinion? Julian Assange is far too self-centered to be able to form a coherent worldview, and for that reason is unable to act in an altruistic way in any sphere, particularly an area where he holds immense power and is surrounded by deferential staff members. He's morally responsible for damage caused by WikiLeaks's release of raw data over the Internet . . . but this opinion isn't why you read this, is it?

So (channeling Master Yoda as you read this), go think you should; what you have learned, use; and your own informed opinion have already!

Third Dump

Risk Management

5
Risky Business

DANIEL CLARKSON FISHER

In a post written in early 2017 for Lawfare—the national security-focused blog of the Brookings Institution and the Lawfare Institute—Jack Goldsmith, political appointee in the George W. Bush administration and professor at Harvard Law School, asks an admittedly provocative question: "Is WikiLeaks different from the *New York Times*?"

Goldsmith observes that WikiLeaks has had a tremendous influence on how newsrooms gather, handle, and report on anonymous leaks, and he doubts there are material differences between WikiLeaks and the *New York Times* with respect to publishing truthful information in the era of doxing. (*Doxing* is the practice of revealing identifying information about someone online, such as real names, addresses, workplaces, and phone numbers.)

In fact, WikiLeaks itself has never published any material that has been shown to be false. Unlike WikiLeaks, the "Grey Lady" that is the *New York Times*, and other print newspapers, apply an editorial filter, which ensures that they're not only more cautious about what they publish than WikiLeaks, but also makes them qualitatively different information organizations. So, *is* WikiLeaks different from the *New York Times*? To Goldsmith's way of thinking, yes and no.

Because of this generally acknowledged blurriness, public figures the world over have continually struggled to position WikiLeaks within the news media landscape. Even a cursory search through headlines reflects a fairly enormous range of perspectives about Julian Assange's outfit.

At one end of the spectrum lies former FBI Director James Comey, who has said that much of WikiLeaks has nothing to do with legitimate news-gathering, but is about nothing more than releasing classified information in order to damage the United States of America. At the other end of the spectrum are Noam Chomsky, Daniel Ellsberg, Slavoj Žižek, Edward Snowden, and many other intellectuals, artists, dissidents, and activists, who have signed an open letter to Donald Trump, saying that "a threat to WikiLeaks's work—which is publishing information protected under the First Amendment—is a threat to all free journalism," and if the US Department of Justice is permitted to convict a publisher for its journalistic work, then "all free journalism can be criminalized."

Between these ends of the spectrum lie quite a few positions struggling to reconcile with varying degrees of thoughtfulness the seeming contradictions which WikiLeaks has presented to us.

And yet, if it feels as if our culture continues to struggle with how to think about the publication of truthful but secret information that concerns public affairs, perhaps it's because of our obstinate insistence on comparing organizations that themselves have articulated appreciably distinct mission statements, value systems, and practices.

Consider that, on the "About" page of their official website, WikiLeaks states that its organization combines "high-end security technologies with journalism and ethical principles." They go on to explain in great detail how their hybrid methods are similar to, but also distinct from, those used in mainstream professional journalism, and while they describe their personnel as journalists, they also note that they provide "a new model of journalism."

Despite such caveats, the organization is perpetually held to standards that it hasn't necessarily set for itself. In certain respects, this is absolutely fair play. If WikiLeaks wants to be considered as legitimate a news source as some place like the *New York Times*, the *Washington Post*, or the *Guardian*, then it should be evaluated with the same yardstick. At the same time, however, if we only apply outside standards, then some basic information that might actually help us to resolve our concerns about releasing private, secret, or classified information will elude us.

For example, how many actually know what WikiLeaks's stated principles are? Shouldn't we be clear about how WikiLeaks's espoused dictates of conscience are and are *not* distinct from those of professional journalists before we compare and contrast the organization itself with others? Shouldn't examining that information be part of thinking through the issues raised by WikiLeaks? Moreover, given the various controversies that have swirled around the organization, it might also be useful to ask, are they acting in accord with their *own* moral code?

Any consideration of these questions must include an examination of one particularly crucial resource. Laura Poitras's 2016 documentary *Risk*, made over the course of several years, includes unprecedented access to WikiLeaks and its founder Julian Assange. Neither WikiLeaks nor Assange participated in the other high-profile documentary about them, Alex Gibney's 2013 film *We Steal Secrets: The Story of WikiLeaks*.

With Poitras at the helm, we're assured that both Assange and his organization get a fair hearing from her critical analysis—her Pulitzer Prize, Polk Award, and Best Documentary Oscar all attest to her journalistic and documentary *bona fides*. In addition, her own credentials as a badass muckraker evince an important sympathy with the broader principles on which WikiLeaks's work is based. Among other things, Poitras was one of the journalists responsible for bringing Edward Snowden's revelations to light, and in 2015 she sued the US Department of Justice, the Department of Homeland Security, and the Office of the Director of National Intelligence after several Freedom of Information Act (FOIA) requests regarding the rationale behind years of harassment were ignored.

Poitras, then, is able to offer a portrait of WikiLeaks and Assange that necessarily and usefully oscillates between informed points of view. A close, careful, and critical reading of *Risk*, alongside other supporting materials, can help us to answer some of the large and important questions about WikiLeaks, journalistic ethics, and integrity. Indeed, Poitras's movie brings clarity here to a degree that's unmatched by other resources. With help from the documentary, we can suss out WikiLeaks's ethics, compare and contrast them with the ethics of mainstream journalism, and assess the organization's professional integrity according to the criteria they themselves have elucidated.

Traditional Journalistic Ethics

While there exists some variety in terms of the best practices articulated by different media outlets, the Society of Professional Journalists' Code of Ethics delineates four core values that are shared universally among news organizations, at least in theory.

The first is to "seek truth and report it." In their view, a professional journalist should be both accurate and fair, but also honest and courageous in the gathering, interpretation, and reporting of information. This includes not only ensuring the facts are correct, identifying sources whenever possible, and promoting open and civil discourse, but also being vigilant about holding to account those with power, while also giving "voice to the voiceless," embracing the Fourth Estate's duty to be the watchdogs over public affairs, and granting access to relevant source material when appropriate.

Second, "minimize harm." Among other things, this requires considering not only the consequences of releasing personal information and the long-term implications of having that information widely available to the public for many, many years. It also requires care in not pandering to the public just because it makes good copy.

Third, "act independently." In part, this involves avoiding conflicts of interest where possible and, where not, disclosing those conflicts. In addition, acting independently means identifying those materials provided by outside sources and separating news from things like advertising.

Finally, professional journalists should "be accountable and transparent." Accountability and transparency demand that journalists explain their decisions and methods to the public, while encouraging a dialogue with them about those practices. Part of what this involves is responding to questions about things such as accuracy and fairness in reporting, owning up to and correcting any errors, explaining these corrections, all in a timely fashion. Moreover, accountability and transparency require that journalists expose unethical behavior within journalism itself, even within their own organizations. After all, these are the standards that journalists seek to hold others to, so it makes sense to hold themselves to the same standards.

Wiki-Ethics

For their part, WikiLeaks has no explicitly stated, prominently placed code of ethics on their website. In this respect, they certainly fit the profile of an outlet that falls under the heading of the *Fifth Estate* (once understood to include underground, countercultural, and outlier publications, but now expanded to include web-based platforms like blogging and social media), rather than the Fourth Estate of traditional mass media. So, it seems fitting that Bill Condon's 2013 biopic about WikiLeaks, starring Benedict Cumberbatch as Julian Assange, is titled *The Fifth Estate*.

However, we do find a set of ethics implicit on the "About" page, and some principles are clearly spelled out at points throughout the document there. WikiLeaks calls itself a not-for-profit media organization dedicated to bringing important news and information to the public. It's made up not only of accredited journalists, but software programmers, network engineers, and volunteers, among others. Its expressed principles include the defense of freedom of speech, and thus of the press to publish such speech, as well as "the improvement of our common historical record and the support of the rights of all people to create new history."

The organization specifically cites the *Universal Declaration of Human Rights* as the basis of this ethos, citing Article 19 as inspiration for the work of their journalists and volunteers. As written in the *Declaration*, that article reads: "Everyone has the right to freedom of opinion and expression; this right includes freedom to hold opinions without interference and to seek, receive and impart information and ideas through any media and regardless of frontiers." WikiLeaks notes their agreement, saying they "seek to uphold this and the other Articles of the Declaration."

They're also especially passionate about getting the "unvarnished truth" to the public, arguing that if publishing improves transparency, and transparency creates a better society, then a robust and engaged media is one of the things that "leads to reduced corruption and stronger democracies in all society's institutions, including government, corporations and other organizations." The impetus here is that public awareness of otherwise unaccountable and secretive institutions forces those institutions to consider the ethical implications of their actions. In other words, the risks of being revealed are singularly effective in combating "conspiracy, corruption, exploitation and oppression."

Turning the tables in this way depends on not just the editorial independence and willing participation of media organizations, but also the "principled leaking" of whistleblowers. This being the case, WikiLeaks speaks of their commitment to developing and improving a "harm minimization procedure." They also outline how their technology ensures the anonymity of those who want to leak information to them, and make other security recommendations for those looking to pass documents to the organization.

In addition, because WikiLeaks isn't motivated by making a profit, they work co-operatively with other media rather than competing with them. For example, they have released documents in collaboration with such news organizations as the *New York Times*, the *Guardian*, *Der Spiegel*, *Le Monde*, and *El País*.

The organization is also committed to releasing materials in full as often as possible, and not just for transparency's sake, but under the belief that making documents freely available will expand both analysis and commentary by all media: "Other journalists may well see an angle or detail in the document that we were not aware of in the first instance."

Placing them alongside each other, we can see significant overlap between the mandates of traditional journalism and WikiLeaks's proclaimed goals, but also distinct differences. For example, both think of themselves as having a special responsibility to the public. Traditional journalism, however, tends to give more weight to a balance of opinions and perspectives than WikiLeaks, which is unabashedly anti-authoritarian in its orientation. Both make a priority of sharing documents and other materials whenever possible, but part company on the need to identify sources. WikiLeaks articulates an exemplary, uncompromising stance with regards to organizational independence, while traditional journalism is far more articulate about issues of self-assessment and institutional management.

Further complicating matters is WikiLeaks's enormous and undeniable influence on the profession of journalism broadly. In addition to feeding mainstream news organizations, WikiLeaks has contributed vital technological tools as well. As Poitras said in an interview on *Charlie Rose*:

> WikiLeaks was founded in 2006, and I think [Assange] understood before a lot of people how the internet was going to change global politics and how it was going to change journalism, both for better and for worse . . . He also understood that, for journalists, [with regards to] the job that we do, to protect sources, it's not enough to say, I'm not going to testify, because with the powers of surveillance that we now have, you [also] need anonymous tools. You need to be able to provide a way to give security to sources. So he did all these things, and he created what's called an anonymous dropbox, so a source can drop information without saying who they are . . . Now almost every news room, I think in the country now, has a similar dropbox.

Traditional journalism and WikiLeaks may not see eye-to-eye on everything, but it would be unreasonable for the one to suggest that nothing important has been learned from the other. At the very least, WikiLeaks has shown traditional journalism how to approach the new *technological* realities of their job.

Yes and No

To best understand and properly assess WikiLeaks, we're required to temper our dogmatism. Merely holding the organization to orthodox standards of journalism fails at intellectual fair-mindedness. In keeping with the movie's title, though, we must also recognize the *risk* that comes with the unorthodox.

Risk throws down the gauntlet right in the opening scene. Assange pours three drinks, one for himself, another for WikiLeaks colleague Sarah Harrison, and a third passed in the direction of the camera: "Laura." Right away, we're presented with something that may strike some professionals as heretical. Doesn't this moment betray a rapport or insider status that's at odds with journalistic "objectivity"?

On the one hand, the documentary filmmaker doesn't operate from the same code of ethics as journalists. Theirs is a big tent, with room enough for everything from the *cinéma vérité* of Chris Hegedus and D.A. Pennebaker to the fictitious interventions of Werner Herzog to the aesthetically beautiful re-enactments of Errol Morris to the polemical comic stylings of Michael Moore. On the other hand, it's probably safe to say that documentarians boozing with their subjects is not something we're used to seeing in nonfiction cinema. To be sure, these first images suggest that doing justice to this particular subject requires venturing into relatively uncharted waters.

Fortunately, Poitras is up to the task of navigating the chop. *Risk* demonstrates in its unconventional strategies that the director clearly comprehends what she needs to do if she's going to offer a genuinely robust documentary. One of her main techniques is to acknowledge that she's no fly on the wall. Instead, she offers through voice-over her honest and unfiltered take as both a documentarian and someone sympathetic to WikiLeaks's larger cause. Sometimes the impressions she shares are cautiously appreciative: "Julian runs the organization like an intelligence agency: using code names, denial and deception, compartmentalization. He's teaching me things about secrecy I didn't realize I needed to learn."

Elsewhere, she's more critical. Explaining her decision not to work with WikiLeaks on the Snowden revelations, Poitras relates a phone conversation that she had with Assange: "He is furious and feels betrayed. He wants me to give him NSA documents and accused me of dividing the community by not publishing with WikiLeaks. I tell him I can't be his source. I don't tell him that I don't trust him. He's still yelling when I hang up the phone." Poitras, along with her colleagues Glenn Greenwald, Ewen MacAskill, and Barton Gellman, ultimately published with the *Guardian* and *Washington Post* and won the 2014 Pulitzer Prize for Public Service.

In terms of its method of operation, Poitras's biggest concern with WikiLeaks is the lack of a certain editorial discretion. As she tells Charlie Rose: "Where my questions come in are decisions not to redact certain types of information . . . things that are personal information, for instance. That is not newsworthy." She cites the example of the DNC leaks, saying, "he published everything, and not everything was newsworthy." Redaction becomes even more important in cases involving active military operations, or other situations in which lives hang in the balance. You could reasonably ask, then: Might redaction and thoughtful curation complement WikiLeaks's efforts to develop a harm minimization procedure?

Poitras's criticism here is powerful because elsewhere in the movie she goes out of her way to show us the ways in which WikiLeaks has been a positive force. For instance, she shows Jacob Appelbaum, a former developer with the Tor Project and spokesperson for WikiLeaks, righteously calling out tech company representatives and government officials for their failure to stand up against censorship on the Internet in the aftermath of 2011's Egyptian revolution.

In addition, we're shown excerpts from "Collateral Murder," video footage of the July 12th 2007 Baghdad airstrikes leaked to WikiLeaks by Chelsea Manning. The shocking footage shows US firepower killing at least a dozen people, among them two Reuters reporters and Iraqi civilians. "Collateral Murder" first made WikiLeaks a household name and also started Poitras on her journey documenting the organization. As she tells Rose: "For me as somebody who had been documenting post-9/11 America, I thought this was really important information that we needed to know about US foreign policy and wars."

Risk seems to defend WikiLeaks against charges that the organization was a witting (or unwitting) accomplice to Russian hackers with the 2016 DNC leaks. We see key moments from Comey's appearance before the Senate Judiciary Committee in which he testifies that an "intermediary" was used by the Russian government. This seems to confirm Assange's insistence that his source isn't a "state actor." Speaking with Rose about this, Poitras says, "You, tomorrow, could receive an anonymous manila envelope with Trump's tax returns . . . It's newsworthy, you verify it. Do you withhold it? No. I mean, that's what reporters do, so I think there is often a double standard when it comes to WikiLeaks." In another moment that complicates the liberal case against WikiLeaks, filmed in 2011, Assange tries to alert then–Secretary of State Hillary Clinton of a data breach at WikiLeaks that could have had adverse effects for the State Department.

Nevertheless, what Edward Snowden has called WikiLeaks's "hostility to even modest curation" is a dealbreaker for Poitras. But it's only one of two dysfunctional elements that *Risk* reveals. The other involves the bullying, abuse, and sexual misconduct that Poitras observes within the WikiLeaks community and which has been amply reported on in other places. Both Assange and Appelbaum have been accused of sexual impropriety, and the movie certainly shows us two men who have trouble talking to and about women. We see scene after scene of Assange aggravating those who are trying to get him to see that his way of addressing the allegations is hugely problematic.

Another scene shows Appelbaum leading a surveillance training for Muslim women activists in Tunis, and using the spectacularly ill-advised metaphor of "safe sex" to explain principles of web security. Toward the end of the film, Poitras admits to having been briefly involved in a consensual sexual relationship with Appelbaum. She further shares that when she asked him to be interviewed about this issue for the movie, he declined. "He wants the film to have a different ending," Poitras says. "So do I." Moments like these inadvertently show us why it is that a group like the Society of Professional Journalists would make it a point to say in their code of ethics that a journalist's responsibility to expose unethical conduct in journalism includes such conduct within their own organization, and that it's important that they adhere to the same standards they expect of others.

So, is WikiLeaks acting in accord with its own ethics? Coming full circle, *Risk* suggests that the answer is "yes and no." On the one hand, their standards and practices are clearly distinguishable from those of professional journalists, so deviations from traditional norms don't necessarily equal transgression. On the other hand, *Risk* often shows us an organization that's struggling to abide by its own founding principles, and badly in need of an unambiguously defined code of ethics.

"Most people who have very strong, principled stances don't survive for long, actually," Assange tells the director early on. "We want them to survive for long, but they don't survive for long." The trick, he explains, is to "understand the medium-term or the long-term goal in principle, and not corrupt your principles in the short term, but be quite willing to balance one for another in order to actually survive the moment."

Risk could very much be read as an examination of this belief in practice, as well as a contemplation on its possibilities and problems. In the final analysis, both audiences and WikiLeaks themselves would do well to heed not only the affirmations but especially the criticisms of Poitras. No one else has ever taken such extraordinary pains to understand the organization both from within and without.

The "Poitras test" that is *Risk* offers a vital institutional review at a point in history when we desperately need more thoughtful, careful, even-handed, and cool-headed analyses of entities such as WikiLeaks.

6
That's a Problem for You, Not Us

David LaRocca

New York Times journalist Scott Shane recently asked: "Is there something particularly American about leaking? Some national allergy to protecting government secrets?" His specific interest is the cultural habits that might provide an answer to these questions, and he finds one reply in a distinctively American political testament: the First Amendment.

Steven Aftergood, Director of the Project on Government Secrecy at the Federation of American Scientists, puts it this way: "To sum up what distinguishes the United States in a nutshell: It's the First Amendment. The concept of a free press has been integral to the American idea since the country's inception. That's not true even of other democracies. The press here even has the right to be irresponsible, which it sometimes is."

Shane and Aftergood are looking squarely at the culture of leaking, the process of making private—and often secret —information public while attempting to maintain the anonymity of the source of that information. So, what's the *philosophical* significance of the often conflicting set of connections, overlaps, and contradictions between the First

Amendment, the free press, free speech, free expression, secrets, and leaks?

On a certain reading, free speech could be described as an *anarchic* value, the power to correct or even destroy the political "powers that be," powers that could—and might— seek to constrain speech through censorship. In this respect, free speech may be regarded as terrorist-friendly. It's a potential instrument of aggression toward a state, hostile or otherwise. So, are there limits to such speech, or is the right to free speech, as some argue, absolute, to be protected at all costs regardless of its content? Free speech absolutists help put into relief the fact that free speech isn't always for the saying of good and useful things, and yet, they argue, it still must be protected no matter what.

Free Speech Is Not a Moral Doctrine

In the United States, the First Amendment to the Constitution was designed and has been upheld by the Supreme Court to protect speech, whatever speech it may be, on public or government property. Private property, being private, isn't covered by the language of the amendment. It should be held in mind, then, that the First Amendment is an artifact of the state, a *legal* rule or principle, and not a *moral* doctrine. It's a legal regulation on human action, not an ethical ideal or value based on whose content that speech is determined to be morally acceptable or objectionable.

At first blush, the position of the free speech absolutists seems noble (or at the very least, ideologically clear and coherent), and in many cases highly convincing. And yet, a prominent figure—a *cause célèbre* and an *enfant terrible* in one—may give us pause: Julian Assange, and by extension, his organization WikiLeaks.

The reason for pause? Might the absolute protection of free speech *also* become a means for sharing information that may bring harm to other people? We're not talking about just offensive speech, for example, which could offend or hurt someone's feelings or damage someone's reputation, but a disclosure that might imperil someone's life, such as revealing the identity of clandestine CIA agents, classified nuclear launch codes, or other covert information that's essential to the security and defense of the state and its citizens.

While there has been a lot of press recently on the right to speak freely without censorship by figures such as Charles Murray, Milo Yiannopoulos, Ann Coulter, and Rebecca Tuvel—all of them, it should be noted, within an *academic* context and some at public universities, others at private colleges—we must consider the ways in which the sharing of certain bits of government and military information may be *categorically* different. If freedom of speech is a legal category, then perhaps we should consider certain kinds of information (what type it is, who possesses it, and how its release might affect the well-being of others) as participating in a *moral* category that is broader than mere legal conventions.

The First Amendment provides a ground for an absolutist ethic, and subsequently we're left to decide how wide a berth the law should have. Censorship, secrecy, classification of documents, and redaction of information are all means of curbing the extent of this otherwise absolutist policy. And yet those who are accused of treason (citizens operating against the state) or terrorism (non-citizens operating against the state) are, we might say, *just trying to fulfill the letter of the law* (in a democracy committed to the First Amendment).

There seems to be an inherent paradox: the very political regime we inhabit, a democracy, and one of its most prized policies, the First Amendment, cultivate the kind of absolutism we seem to see in Assange. One possible response to this paradox is that WikiLeaks, with Assange at its helm, provides an instance of epistemological consistency while simultaneously revealing a potentially disastrous moral failing.

For context, I draw on Laura Poitras's documentary movie, *Risk* (2017), where she notes that Assange and WikiLeaks's staff are under a secret US grand jury investigation for espionage and conspiracy. As if in reply, Assange articulates his ambitions for the organization he founded and runs, in recent years while in exile within the Ecuadorian embassy in London:

> I don't believe in martyrs. There are some very rare exceptions that people should be martyred, but I think people should certainly take risks—understand carefully what the risks are. Sometimes the risks can be very high, but the opportunity can be extremely high.

Assange, as befits his paranoid style, rarely makes clear the objects of his descriptions. To what risks does he allude? What opportunity does he have in mind? Whatever the actual answers, it's sufficiently evident, not in the least for the aggressive treatment by the US government, that Assange is taking risks and seeking opportunities.

In a rare moment of lucidity and disclosure, Assange opines in *Risk*:

> It has been my long-term belief that what advances us as a civilization is the entirety of our understanding—what human institutions are actually like. And at the moment, we are severely lacking in information from big, secretive organizations that have such a role in shaping how we all live.

Here Assange throws his chips down on the side of the information absolutists, those who would say that we ought to aim at revealing the *entirety* of whatever may lay hidden. Thus, Assange takes as his goal not so much the moral impulse of the whistleblower but something more like the lighthouse keeper, who wishes to shine a spotlight on the shadows, revealing the dangerous, destructive rocks that lie unseen near the shore and in the shallows. Perhaps light-pointing aims to illuminate the working of a "deep" (or dark) state.

Ruthless Pragmatism

Nevertheless, Assange re-frames his epistemological absolutism—namely, that free speech is the gold standard—with a worry about the ethical status of persons: "Institutions, the most powerful institutions—from the CIA to News Corporation—are all organized using technical young people. What does it mean when all those technical young people adopt a certain value system? And that they are in an institution where they do not agree with the value system? And yet, actually, their hands are on the machinery." Again, with vague language Assange doesn't tell us what that value system is. In fact, might it not be the case that we find ourselves in a rather *amoral* space, where these "technical young people"—who have spent their lives online, before private screens—no longer have genuine ethical training through intimate socialization with other human beings, but instead operate out of the bounds of *any* previously constraining moral system? Assange's amphiboly makes it possible to read "certain value system" as *no* value system, or perhaps, an anti-value system.

When we finally do hear Assange describe his relation to the absolutism that underwrites his vision for WikiLeaks, we may be chastened, for it doesn't appear to be the "certain value system" we were expecting:

Most people who have very strong principled stances don't survive for long, actually. You want them to survive for long, but they don't survive for long. And do much at the same time. There are many times in WikiLeaks's evolution where I've had to be ruthlessly pragmatic. So it is to understand the medium term or the long term goal and principle, but in fact not corrupt your principles in the short term but be quite willing to balance one for another in order to actually survive the moment.

With *Risk*, we may see the way in which an "information wants to be free" First Amendment–style absolutism comes into conflict with the so-called "ruthlessly pragmatic" approach Assange has at times had to adopt. WikiLeaks may be famous—or infamous—for being absolutist, and yet Assange's strategies of leaking information may be better described as relativist, subjectivist, amoral, cynical, and even tactical. As such, we're left to contend with the ways in which not just WikiLeaks and Assange, but any organization or agent that wishes to take up this mantle, may put themselves beyond accountability.

Looking back to touchstones of the free press—even ones that preceded but no doubt informed the generation of the First Amendment on American soil, such as John Milton's *Areopagitica* (1644)—recall Aftergood's notion that the free press in America has the right to be irresponsible and sometimes is. Do WikiLeaks and its leader, Assange, exhibit a contemporary case of such moral delinquency? If so, is it (or should we take it to be) a *right* to be careless with classified information? As we see in the cases of academics noted above, we may be eager to defend these thinkers in their pursuit of truths, even if as yet unknown or unproven, and even if potentially contrary to prevailing trends and mores, and yet, we may not be nearly as full of conviction in defending them if we believe that in their disclosure of information (for example, if they pursued their research and publication) they might *harm* others—in real ways, such as by imprisonment or torture or death.

A case in point: fundamental scientific research on human beings is regularly thwarted because of ethical concerns about the mistreatment of such human subjects in a laboratory setting. This is the case for both behavioral studies, such as in psychology, and in biomedical settings, such as in the study of oncology or neuroscience and, for example, in the debate among geneticists about whether or not to pursue heritable changes to DNA with technologies such as CRISPR.

In *all* of these cases, academic or scientific objectives don't overrule the mandates of *respect* for persons, meaning the protection of their dignity *as* persons. Academics may appeal to the First Amendment as an instrument to combat this limitation, and yet a credo as ancient as the Hippocratic oath—do no harm—seems sufficient to impede potentially untoward, if well-meaning, intellectual pursuits.

"Free speech" as it is known in the academy (as a function of the pursuit of truth, especially one protected by the institution known as tenure) may be, as I'm suggesting, categorically distinct from the claims of "free speech" promulgated by WikiLeaks and Assange. For one thing, WikiLeaks and Assange aren't conducting original research. They aren't sharing hard-won discoveries. Rather, they're sharing other people's property (including intellectual property) and information that may damage persons and, thus, well-being. Even if we overlook the description of this act as larceny, we may say that the theft is secondary to the harm of *sharing* the stolen property. Attorneys for WikiLeaks may want to argue that the organization is merely a conduit for information, but the act of releasing that information can be—in the case of vital, classified data—morally catastrophic precisely because it's potentially harmful to other human persons.

Promulgated on a sufficiently mass scale such as WikiLeaks is known for and with a sense for possible, or even likely, deleterious effects, we can imagine such releases being the moral equivalent of crimes against humanity.

Free Speech Hero or Hacktivist Anti-Hero?

Observing the contradiction inherent in Assange's position isn't meant to be personal, an *ad hominem* logical fallacy, but rather, is drawn so we may see an *impersonal* pattern, namely, how the *idea* of free speech as the unbridled release of *any* information whatsoever is itself potentially hazardous. Yet, since our subject is WikiLeaks and Assange, we can keep them in mind as representative of *a particular reading* of free speech, one that may be claimed to possess logical "principles" and yet mask an underlying ideological motivation.

We're left, then, to wonder whether Assange is a true ideologue who seeks to exercise an absolutist principle of free speech, for example, in the service of cultivating the means for sharing "the entirety of our understanding," or whether he's better defined as an anarchist hacker who aims to fill the role of institutional, governmental, and organizational gadfly. Even though he says he's acting out of principle—we must presume the principle of free speech is aligned, in this case, with the principle that "information wants to be free"—he, in fact, seems to be channeling and continuing his youthful venture, the International Subversives, a hacking group he began and operated, and for which he was later prosecuted.

At an early, tense moment in the Laura Poitras movie, *Risk*, Assange's aide-de-camp, Sarah Harrison, calls the US Department of State and asks, "Can I speak with Hillary Clinton, please?" Assange sits nearby, watching Harrison intently, feeding her lines. Harrison warns the proxy that a trove of State Department data is about to be released, "not by us." On a later occasion, when a State Department lawyer calls back and Assange makes clear "this is a problem for you, not us," we see the shifting landscape of Assange's "ruthless pragmatism" in action. This scene, among many others in the movie (and beyond it), illustrates Assange thinking in real time about *strategy*, about opportunity, not about policy or principle. We're given a chance to see how the name WikiLeaks may itself be strategic—directing our attention to the art and practice of leaking—when the name of his earlier operation, the International Subversives, may better capture the nature of what Assange and his team undertake to do and to accomplish.

To move forward with an understanding of Assange's project—in particular, with WikiLeaks as a means of *justified* free expression—let's become attuned to the *moral* reasoning of some of the free speech absolutists. For starters, those who would appear to be censoring speech are denied the position of rational interlocutors who may be making a cogent argument of their own. When Andrew Sullivan commented on free speech as it's known—or curbed—on academic campuses, he remarked that the notion of intersectionality "is not an argument. It's a religion, a kind of secular religion. If you're on campus, you have to believe certain things, or you are a heretic."

Referring to Charles Murray's fate at Middlebury College—where he was shouted off the stage and later assaulted (along with Allison Stanger, who suffered a concussion)—Sullivan concludes: "What you saw here is the burning of a heretic." William Deresiewicz sustains Sullivan's point when he writes, "The fundamental questions that a college education ought to raise—questions of individual and collective virtue, of what it means to be a good person and a good community—are understood to have been settled. The assumption, on elite college campuses, is that we are already in full possession of the moral truth. This is a religious attitude. It is certainly not a scholarly or intellectual attitude."

To broaden the scope of the Sullivan-Deresiewicz position, pushing the purview beyond the cloister of academe, Sam Harris states that freedom of speech is not merely

one among many different values. It really is the master value. Because it's the only corrective to human stupidity. It's the only mechanism by which we can improve our society. It's the value that allows us to improve our other values.

Harris's interlocutor, Jordan B. Peterson (famed for his resistance to Bill C-16, the now-passed Canadian law protecting the rights of LGBT persons) claims that freedom of speech is "the fundamental value upon which our entire cultural edifice is predicated."

Meanwhile, and for a long time, literary critic and legal scholar, Stanley Fish, has claimed that free speech isn't an *academic* value, and it never was. What is it, then? For Fish, accuracy of speech, completeness of speech, relevance of speech: "Each of these values is directly related to the goal of academic inquiry: getting a matter of fact right." Fish goes on to conclude that the academy should neither be condoned as a place for political speech (that's an "extra-curricular" activity), nor should it be mistaken for a democracy (it is, he points out, at least ideally, a meritocracy). In summary, then, there are certain types of speech that should neither be allowed nor defended on university campuses (political speech being one), and beyond that a citizen's sense that he or she has a "right" to say whatever he or she believes (true or not) misses the crucial fact that the academy is designed precisely to test speech, to take care with it, in effect, to *police* it; academics call this by the more sober-sounding locution "peer review." Academics, it turns out, on the whole, are free to say very little.

Adapting Fish's argument about the value of free speech in the academy to the case of WikiLeaks, I claim that free speech isn't a *democratic* value either, and it never was. Such a seemingly counterintuitive assertion finds its evidence in the fact that free speech, in its rigorous, absolutist sense, is antithetical to the protection and maintenance of government secrets. Like the academy, the government relies on peer vetting, for example, by those with specialized training, by those with security clearances, and so forth.

We may immediately find ourselves troubled by "the cult of the expert" (much as we find it in academe) but, unlike university life, most of the experts in government remain unknown to the public. Even if such secret experts have power of which we are suspicious (as Assange clearly is), we aren't in a position to assess that status either way. Indeed, this could even be said when secrets *are* leaked, where cultural critics, journalists, policy makers, political pundits, and the like, rack their brains trying to understand what it all means. An information dump amounts to just that, a wasteland of immeasurably large scope lacking coherence that, therefore, endlessly defers the drawing of cogent, verifiable conclusions.

Information Wants to Be Handled Properly

To return to the scene in *Risk* in which Assange and his affiliates stand on the brink of such an information dump, we should take stock of the kind of position this puts Assange in with respect to his theory of free speech as well as to his moral obligations to his fellow man. Even as Harrison and Assange declare (blithely it seems to me) that the imminent discharge of secret documents is "a problem for you, not us," it must be noted how that release is very much a problem for them. At the very minimum, if they're part of the citizenry negatively affected by the release, then it *is* their problem. At this level of basic narcissistic self-regard, the leak may damage Assange and his associates. No doubt, Assange has his reply to this in the language of "risk." And so we're returned to his ruthlessly utilitarian calculus (the recipe for which only he knows—that elemental bit of information will *not* be leaked).

So let's say, then, that just because you may come into possession of information, it doesn't mean (by some sort of anthropomorphic legerdemain) that "information wants to be free." That's a myth in the guise of a justification. Rather, if we're going to think of the context of a democratic citizenry and its responsibilities to itself (and even *other* democracies), we would be better off claiming that "information wants to be handled properly"—for accuracy, completeness, and relevance, to echo Fish—by those who are trained to handle it.

The conspiratorial, or merely cynical, comeback is always, "But who watches the watchmen?" Again, James Madison and his brethren, even in the late eighteenth century, had their own paranoias and asked the same question. In short measure, the Constitution and the organization of government is supposed to have a system of "checks and balances" that operates *on behalf of* a broader public discourse. Turned another way, however, we might simply observe that the Constitution, by and large, orchestrates a rather anti-democratic regime. Why is this? Precisely because mob rule, of which WikiLeaks is a digital manifestation, may degenerate, in time, into tyranny. But who said *that* first? Not the designers of the US Constitution, and certainly not Assange, but rather someone whose works found a place on the framers' bookshelves.

Plato (427–347 B.C.E.), in his dialogue *The Republic*, worries about a certain type of person who, he says, "frequently goes in for politics and bounces up and says whatever enters his head." Moreover, Plato argues that a government that accustoms its people to too much freedom will make its citizens "so sensitive that they chafe at the slightest suggestion of servitude and will not endure it." He draws the conclusion that the probable outcome of too much freedom is "only too much slavery in the individual and the state."

Democracy, in other words, becomes dangerous *to itself* when it becomes *too* free, because it thereby exposes itself to tyrannical impulses that capitalize on that freedom in order to discharge and dislodge the structures of "checks and balances" and usurp power. Indeed, in such an anything-goes, say-what-you-will world of fake news and fact-free zones, the tyrant hears his siren call and steps onto the stage. (Andrew Sullivan, to his credit, speculated that Plato's diagnosis of democracy's fragility was upon us—and he did it in the Spring of 2016.)

To keep our thinking grounded in practical reality, allow me to conclude with some tractable specifics. Award-winning journalist, Tim Weiner, has argued that the CIA— a government agency that relies on the making and keeping of secrets—needs the free press, otherwise it would devolve into the KGB or even MI5 with its use of D-notices (official requests to news editors not to publish or broadcast information for reasons of national security). Yet, when we hear Weiner speak with fellow journalist Malcolm Gladwell, we must draw a conclusion neither Gladwell nor Weiner articulate but which both underwrite, namely, that the free press is not *free*, or not *entirely* or *absolutely* free. Rather, the relationship between these clandestine services and journalists is, well, a "dance," or perhaps better a series of nuanced judgment calls that *depend on* secrecy, discretion, and decency (as well as the virtues of accuracy, completeness, and relevance already mentioned). Gladwell focuses on showing us how the CIA and, more particularly, the *New York Times*, but also more generally we as citizens, wronged the asset referred to as "Al Pacino" by putting his status—and his photograph—on page one of the newspaper. Was it a surprise to the *New York Times* that soon after they published this information, the asset was killed?

This is a haunting and sad cautionary tale, but it also serves as a veritable illustration of the fact that we're careless—perhaps lethally so—when we take umbrage at limitations on speech. It's the "chill" that people resent, the "muzzle," the "gag," and other violent metaphors regularly invoked when people feel they aren't free to say whatever they want to say, and so invoke the presumed trump card, "It's a free country." And yet, you can say whatever you want, or release whatever photographs of assets, and the like, because you believe that free speech is an absolute value, but then people are injured or die, or if they survive, their careers may be ruined, as with the second Bush administration's outing of Valerie Plame as a CIA agent.

And so we arrive at one of the lessons that philosophy can teach us about WikiLeaks: we should *want* our journalists to withhold information, even if it's well-sourced, when agencies like the CIA indicate that harm may come if that information is released. Call this a Hippocratic Oath for the journalist set. And we can make a parallel argument about anonymous sources, who are perhaps rightly regarded as their own kind of secret agents.

Journalists know the names of their sources but will cite them in the published work as anonymous (as a legitimate bid for their protection). Imagine instead that, in the name of full disclosure, free speech, and freedom of information, we insisted that anonymous sources be outed. Think of how paltry, how erroneous, indeed how little decent information we would get, if we'd get any at all.

Journalism thrives by anonymity. And because our sense of the truth depends on the methodologies and morals of journalists, so do we.

Assange fails to see that in a robust, functioning democracy, truth and safety depend on secrecy and constraints on speech.

Fourth Dump

Truth Sleuth

7
The Truth, the Whole Truth, and Nothing But the Truth?

Isadora Mosch and
L. Brooke Rudow-Abouharb

While it may seem obvious that outright lying isn't morally praiseworthy, it's far less clear whether active truth-telling is always praiseworthy, much less morally obligatory. We tend to think that more truth and transparency is better, especially when it comes to politics, but the overabundance of information, fake news, alternative facts, and the emergence of entities such as WikiLeaks have thrust questions about truth and truth-telling methods to the forefront of public debate.

The Good, the Bad, and the Ugly

One of the highest purported aims of philosophy is truth. Each of philosophy's disciplines attempts to give some correct account of whatever its subject matter may be. What is beauty? What is love? What is the nature of reality? Each question struggles for a *true* answer, and the greatest use of human rationality is to discover that answer. It's no wonder that the philosopher Immanuel Kant (1724–1804) famously argued that to spread false information, to lie, is an egregious moral failure. Kant's moral philosophy, sometimes called *deontology*, requires that, regardless of the outcome, it's always morally wrong to lie. You must never lie under any circumstance.

Never? NEVER. But why? Surely there are situations where it's actually morally *better* to lie than to tell the truth, like when the truth hurts. According to Kant, the answer is a resounding "No." Kant's formula of humanity says that we should always treat people as ends in themselves, never merely as means. We should respect people's dignity and not use them to get what we want. When we lie to someone, we use that person as a means to our own end, rather than treating them as an end in themselves.

Treating people merely as a means ignores that they have their own desires and goals, and this breaks the most basic rule of respect for human autonomy. Autonomy means that you can make choices for yourself without being forced, coerced, or manipulated. It's the essence of our humanity. And, in order to make the best and most rational choices for ourselves, we must make those decisions based on things that are true. The liar, therefore, strips another of their autonomy, thereby violating their humanity. Thus, lying is always morally wrong.

Lies are one thing, but truth-telling is another. Kant says only that we have a moral obligation, or duty, *not to lie*. So, what about the positive side of things? Should we always tell the truth? Unfortunately, Kant tells us very little in this regard, and considering it carefully, humans have a pretty complicated relationship with truth. Although we recognize that, when asked directly, we ought not to lie, we tend to be quite reserved about simply *dispensing* the truth, and for good reason.

As the saying goes, the truth hurts. But the truth hurting doesn't necessarily mean that it's a bad thing. We often need to confront uncomfortable truths in order to change and become better people. If I have a habit of interrupting people, I need to know this so that I can stop doing it. It probably hurts to hear it, but becoming a better listener and friend is a net benefit to me. So, even though the truth may hurt, it's sometimes a good thing. However, when we start to abuse the truth, using it selectively or irrelevantly, it can be a genuine moral harm by manipulating and ultimately undermining autonomy. According to Kant, the truth isn't good because of its intended consequence. We shouldn't judge the morality of any action on the basis of its effects; we should judge it based on its relationship to rationality and autonomy. Thus, if truth-telling violates autonomy, then it's morally wrong.

Selective Truths

A truth is *selective* when what's revealed is true but it's revealed in such a way that it's either incomplete or it obscures other truths. Usually, selectivity is a social necessity. Suppose you're on a first date, and your date asks about your life. While you can't tell this person every detail from every day, you *can* pick and choose which features of your life are relevant to share. It would be off-putting *not* to be selective here! And, almost every information-sharing interaction is like this. We simply can't share everything, so we must cherry-pick truths to suit our needs.

However, selectivity can play a decidedly more malicious role. Sometimes in telling only *some* of the truth, I actually violate someone's autonomy. Suppose someone comes across damning information about both Hillary Clinton and Donald Trump just prior to the 2016 presidential election. This person, being a Trump supporter, reveals only the information about Clinton. Here, selectivity has a more dubious character, one we may characterize as a "lie by omission." Selective truth-telling and lying by omission are two sides of the same coin, because both aim to manipulate how others understand reality.

But, let's be honest. We've all done this because, well, *they aren't really lies.* Omission is a way of selectively *telling the truth* that allows us walk away feeling better about ourselves. We didn't *really* lie, after all. But selectivity strips away the autonomy of the other in the very same ways that a lie does, by undermining the other's ability to make fully realized choices. One solution might seem to be telling the whole truth, to provide an "information dump" that presents all the information. But even if someone tells the whole truth, we may have another problem: *irrelevance.*

Irrelevant Truths

There's a clear-cut way in which truth can be irrelevant: some truth ought not have any bearing on the topic at hand, and it actually serves to *distract* from other, more pertinent, truths. A classic example is an ad hominem argument: a person's character is attacked instead of addressing the main issue.

Remember our source with the intel about Clinton and Trump? Let's say the information about Clinton has no bearing on her fitness to be president, but it's *really* embarrassing. Here, there's no duty to tell the truth, even if it's the whole truth, because it lacks relevance. In fact, it might actually be *wrong* for me to tell this story if, for example, I'm using it to cast her in an unjustifiably negative light with the aim to manipulate the judgments and decisions of potential voters. This highlights the role played by *motive* in evaluating the morality of an action. Just as my motive for telling a selective truth matters, so matters my motive for what *part* of that truth I select.

The truth can also be irrelevant in a more complex way. A truth could potentially matter, but without the surrounding context or relevant knowledge, it's unclear in what ways it actually does matter. Even though, in principle, we have access to an abundance of information, it might be completely *inaccessible* in practice. In fact, this is a significant problem for the technical sciences. It's difficult, if not impossible, to effectively communicate highly complex scientific truths to the public because the public, in general, lacks the relevant vocabulary, knowledge, and context. Indeed, this difficulty is now at the fore of public engagement with climate change science, as it has been in the past with the science surrounding nuclear radiation.

The television show *Adventure Time* highlights this problem when Finn tries to "talk science" with Princess Bubblegum in the episode "Ricardio the Heart Guy":

> FINN: Oh . . . I'm . . . into Zanoits! Th-They're the best!
>
> PRINCESS BUBBLEGUM: Zanoits kill hundreds of thousands of Plantoids a year.
>
> FINN: Oh, no, not the Plantoids!
>
> PRINCESS BUBBLEGUM: Plantoids produce mellotoxin! [*Finn stares.*]
>
> PRINCESS BUBBLEGUM: Mellotoxin kills Zanoits!!
>
> FINN: So, are Zanoits . . . *good* things?

Finn can't get a grasp on what to think about Zanoits because he doesn't know anything about them. You may give me the whole truth, but the whole truth may mean nothing or may mean something scary if I don't really understand it. And yet, this kind of irrelevancy doesn't appear to be a form of manipulation or morally problematic. It's actually a problem inherent to the division of intellectual labor. Where it becomes problematic is the *abuse* of complexity to muddy the truth. Considering climate science, where various organizations take advantage of the subtle differences in research to claim that there's *no consensus* on climate change. Because the layperson has little to no scientific expertise, it becomes difficult to overcome these claims. When I must be told by someone else what something means, complexities can easily be used to undermine my autonomy by leading me to conclusions that are not my own. In other words, they can be used as a means of manipulation.

Once Upon a Time on the Web

It seems as if we could overcome these two abuses of truth. Information has never been so widely available. Yet, they say we've come into a "post-truth" era. How could this be?

Most questions can be resolved within seconds using Internet search engines. We have access to almost every newspaper in the world, and scholarly work at the highest levels is readily available to the layperson. And yet, we suffer from "alternative facts," "fake news," and a proliferation of "evidence" that can confirm whatever crazy ideas someone has (talking to you, flat-earthers!). In the face of all this truth, there seems to be a big problem actually *finding* it. WikiLeaks claims to show the way.

It's no secret that mainstream media are selective in their content, whether this is due to political bias or the simple fact that *some* selectivity can't be avoided. Recall how impossible it is to tell the whole truth about yourself on a date. Selectively presenting the news is an unfortunate side-effect of a world that never stops changing. But, just as a date can *mislead* you with selective half-truths, so can mainstream media. You would think that the twenty-four-hour news cycle would be an antidote to this sort of selectivity, increasing our access to pluralistic information. Even though this minute-by-minute update creates room for more information, inevitably, in order to capture viewers' attention and fill the time, it also provides room for biased commentary and sensationalizing.

Both sides of the party line accuse news sources of being biased and serving some hidden interest. CNN is accused of having a liberal bias, while the *Wall Street Journal* is accused of conservative bias. These accusations of bias aren't based on these news sources presenting false information (Fox News notwithstanding), but rather on *which* truths they are willing to include. Since they are presenting true information, it would seem that some biased cherry-picking isn't all that problematic. However, it can become an echo chamber, in which beliefs are amplified and reinforced (the *echo*) within a closed system (the *chamber*) that doesn't admit new and competing information. Selectivity here ends up catering to what a certain audience already believes and wants to hear, but in doing so, creates a closed feedback loop, giving people what they want instead of what they need.

The information they need is precisely what WikiLeaks claims to provide. It publishes leaks, information that normally wouldn't be available to, or is expressly prohibited from, the public. WikiLeaks prides itself on being the one source of information that has a perfect record for document authentication and resistance to censorship. Essentially, if you are getting information from WikiLeaks, you're getting the truth—*all of it*, they say. When you visit the WikiLeaks website, the leaks are categorized into sets. Clicking one of the sets takes you to a page with a brief description of what type of information the files contain, along with the original files. The sheer amount of information is plainly over-whelming and, in this sense, it's clear that WikiLeaks is upholding its commitment to provide the public with unfettered access to truth.

It seems, then, that WikiLeaks overcomes the ills of mainstream media. Though an individual can (and must) pick and choose which leaks to engage—you can't read them all—they are all there. So, you have to wonder, why all the controversy? Given that WikiLeaks's ultimate goal is to be a voice of truth in a world of censorship, limited access, and thinly-veiled attempts to sway public opinion, and given that they are largely successful in that endeavor, why does WikiLeaks receive such a mixed reception?

Dubious Intentions

In a statement posted on the eve of the 2016 Presidential Election, WikiLeaks responded to some of its critics. The criticism was leveled at WikiLeaks's release of emails between Hillary Clinton, her staff, and members of the Democratic National Committee (DNC). In the wake of the State Department's investigation of Clinton's use of a personal email server, WikiLeaks created a searchable archive of over 30,000 emails and attachments sent to and from Clinton on that server. Shortly after setting up this archive, WikiLeaks began releasing a series of leaked emails from seven staff members of the DNC as well as Clinton's campaign chairman, John Podesta. The emails contained highly controversial and damaging information, including the alleged sabotage of the Bernie Sanders campaign, Clinton's admission to having opposing public and private positions on key issues, and an indication that Clinton was being given debate questions in advance. These damning implications sent the campaign into a tailspin, and the timing is hard to ignore.

The DNC emails were released on July 22nd 2016, just ahead of the Democratic National Convention, and the Podesta emails dropped a mere hour after the release of the "Access Hollywood" tapes—tapes that contain a conversation during which Donald Trump brags about sexually assaulting women. The *New York Times* reported that WikiLeaks founder Julian Assange had timed the release of the leaks intentionally to disrupt Clinton's campaign. The *Times* article suggests that Assange saw Clinton as both a political and personal foe and seemed excited about the coming release of more emails. Assange, however, tells another tale. In his election eve defense statement, Assange positions himself as the righteous bearer of truth. What he says is worth reprinting in part (emphasis ours):

> We publish material given to us *if it is of political, diplomatic, historical or ethical importance and which has not been published elsewhere*. When we have material that fulfills this criteria, we publish. We had information that fit our editorial criteria which related to the Sanders and Clinton campaign (DNC Leaks) and the Clinton political campaign and Foundation (Podesta Emails). No-one disputes the public importance of these publications. It would be unconscionable for WikiLeaks to withhold such an archive from the public during an election.
>
> At the same time, we cannot publish what we do not have. To date, we have not received information on Donald Trump's campaign . . . or any of the other candidates that fulfills our stated editorial criteria.
>
> This is not due to a personal desire to influence the outcome of the election . . . WikiLeaks remains committed to publishing information that informs the public, even if many, especially those in power, would prefer not to see it. WikiLeaks must publish. It must publish and be damned.

Here, Assange attempts to deflect the claim that the releases were timed strategically, claiming that "We publish as fast as our resources will allow and as fast as the public can absorb it."

Timing Is Everything

We're in tricky territory here. The timing of the email leaks is pretty suspect, but we aren't in a great position to determine the truth of the matter. Regardless, we can think about the ethical implications *either way*. If Assange is telling the truth, and WikiLeaks always releases documents as soon as it can, then there doesn't seem to be a moral problem here. The truth exposed was (eventually) complete and relevant, and it would be hard to argue that it could be seen as manipulation. On the other hand, let's say that Assange held the leaks and waited to release them at a time that would be most damaging to Clinton and the DNC or would distract from Trump's indiscretions. If this was his intention, the information dump might make us a bit more uneasy.

For one thing, timing releases would go directly against the principle of immediate release that WikiLeaks proclaims to uphold. Furthermore, it would constitute a form of selectivity. *Even if* WikiLeaks released all of the information they had, it selected particular moments to do so that would stand out in the American consciousness. Rather than truly giving the public the time to absorb it, WikiLeaks set off a series of "truth bombs" that went off one after another until right up to the eve of the election. While this doesn't directly or completely strip away the autonomy of the voter, it does create chaos and confusion that's difficult to navigate. An individual is far more easily pushed when they have nothing solid on which to stand.

Inaccessibly Accessible

We can't be entirely sure whether or not WikiLeaks had a moral slip-up during the 2016 presidential election, so aside from the emails, what information is the public getting? The volume of information is staggering, appearing to be complete, and as Assange said in his defense, it's all politically, diplomatically, historically, and ethically relevant.

Then can't we say that, in general, WikiLeaks is a good thing? Well, remember that even potentially relevant information can turn out to be a problem. If I have no context or background knowledge, something important might mean nothing to me. While WikiLeaks provides file upon file of potentially valuable information, that potentiality is difficult to actualize. WikiLeaks provides an analysis for each set of documents, of course, but this analysis is a step away from the sources that constitute the real contribution that WikiLeaks makes: the *original leaked material*.

Yet, going directly to the original documents themselves, as a layperson, is often pointless. There are often extremely complex reports coupled with insider jargon, and, many times, documents are written in languages other than English. Though the documents are there, there's little I can really do with them. I can read them, but I can't really understand what significance they have. I *need* the analyses. I need someone to interpret them, provide the context surrounding them, and, just like Finn, tell me whether they are good things or bad things.

The end result is that, for the most part, we have to rely on once-removed analyses and descriptions for any sort of clear idea about what the leaks are *about*, what the leaks *say*, and why they *matter*. So even though WikiLeaks says that the leaks are for the public, they are nonetheless decidedly inaccessible to most individual members of the public. Here, the *potential* for manipulation is high, where once again, someone else must tell me what to think.

Yet, we really can't maintain that WikiLeaks is morally wrong for this. They face the same difficulties as our climate scientists above. They are making an attempt to be transparent, even if, by and large, this transparency may not help the average individual by way of direct access. And even though many of the documents are inaccessible, *at least they are there*, and accessible to the minority who *can* bring the tools of analysis to the information. Even though I may not be able to work through the material or read Russian, the community at large can. Thus, there's a net *increase of autonomy* for the community.

This crowd-sourced analysis isn't a perfect system, but having original sources of information available to the public, open for a community of critique and interpretation, is far better than having them hidden behind a "classified" screen. The availability of these censored, classified, or hidden documents paves the way for a system of communal checks and balances that was nearly impossible prior to the emergence of WikiLeaks.

Precariously Perched

So where does all this leave us? As Harry S. Truman said, "Secrecy and a free, democratic government don't mix," and for Kant, truth is a good regardless of the consequences. This holds not only for the small-scale personal interactions we have day to day, but it's part and parcel of Kant's political philosophy, as well. State secrets have no place in a just society, according to Kant, and no matter what might happen, a free society is one whose policy and practice is public. Insofar as WikiLeaks contributes to the publicity of our government, it's a net good.

However, WikiLeaks isn't without its own set of limitations and problems, which seem to regress back to problems associated with mainstream media. Because of the *inaccessibility* of much of the WikiLeaks material, it *has* to be interpreted by someone. If it's interpreted by the media, it falls back into the cycle of the biased selectivity of mainstream media. Therefore, something has to fundamentally change about mainstream media in order for WikiLeaks to be able really to do its job.

If WikiLeaks does the interpreting on its own, it can end up functioning as merely another voice among others. It becomes another news outlet. Moreover, and perhaps more alarming, if Assange himself is *selectively* releasing leaks (by timing their release, for instance), then he is in essence performing the same function as a biased media. WikiLeaks then becomes the stage for Assange to play out his own strategic meddling and advance his personal political agenda.

At its core, then, WikiLeaks itself can regress into just another form of political manipulation, and end up in little better position than the mainstream media it decries. Ultimately, a definitive conclusion about the moral status of WikiLeaks may well be impossible given the limited access we have to the motivations and practices behind the scenes. Nonetheless, one *can* conclude that WikiLeaks teeters in a precarious position between illumination and manipulation, serving the good of a free and democratic society while prone to the dangers of selectivity and bias.

8
Lied to for Your Own Good

FRANK SCALAMBRINO

WikiLeaks and its revelations are, evidently, like an unexpected pregnancy. Before it's here you don't want it, but once it appears you don't want it to go away.

Though the issues and principles involved are as old as government itself, Niccolò Machiavelli (1469–1527), who wrote *The Prince* in 1513, may be seen as popularizing the position that it's not good government policy for government policy to be transparent. Yet, greater levels of transparency are said to protect the people from losing their say in what the United States of America does as a nation, thereby, protecting citizens from the demise of democracy.

Transparency, in other words, supports the kind of "rule by the people" that is associated with American democracy.

Are You Ready to Get Your Hands Dirty?

In Western philosophy, this raises the so-called Problem of Dirty Hands. The basic question of the problem is whether government leaders should (be allowed to) act immorally? Of course, Machiavelli thought that government leaders weren't being very good government leaders if they weren't acting immorally. The reasons for Machiavelli's conclusion are as true today as they were then. Thus, Machiavelli's solution to the problem of dirty hands is subterfuge. In other words, government policy, foreign and domestic, should be immoral, and the government leaders involved in such immorality should use tricks to hide the immorality of their actions from their citizens.

WikiLeaks, however, presents an obstacle to such subterfuge by revealing the actions of governments to its citizens and to the global community. As a result, citizens may come to realize not only that the government may be engaged in immoral activity but also that the people may feel as though they had no say in the matter, or that they have no real say in future foreign and domestic policy.

The issues raised by the WikiLeaks revelations permeate all levels of culture from movies like *Jason Bourne* (2016) to the US presidential election, in which candidate, and now forty-fifth president of the United States, Donald Trump declared "I love WikiLeaks!"

Machiavelli argued that governments actually have a *duty* to their citizens to be immoral. As Stuart Hampshire puts it in his book *Public and Private Morality*: "If one refused to be ruthless in pursuit of objectives in public policy, and refused to use deceit and guile as instruments of policy, one betrayed those who had put their trust in the man who represents them." Deceit and violence, Hampshire argues, are *normal* in the relations between states. It would be wrongheaded of government leaders, according to Machiavelli, to govern according to the moral standards that the citizens use to relate to one another, for example, standards such as equality, fairness, earnestness, and charity. In order for government to be doing its job correctly, it must be *ruthless*.

Machiavelli justifies this position in two different ways, and both are quite simple. First, war is inevitable and, therefore, unavoidable. Second, nations have a duty to secure resources for their citizens. Thus, on the one hand, from at least the time of St. Augustine (354–430) the concept of the Just War has been used to support not only violence against enemies but also pre-emptive violence, which Machiavelli expresses by arguing that "you cannot escape wars, and when you put them off only your opponents benefit." On the other hand, because resources, such as land and oil, are limited, and it's the duty of governments to secure resources for their citizens, some version of "stealing" from foreign nations will eventually be necessary. In this way, Machiavelli prefigures Thomas Hobbes (1588–1679), who held a similar understanding of the natural condition of humanity and therefore the need for a strong state with great latitude in governing itself.

With regard to the first justification, Machiavelli says, "It will always happen that he who is not your ally will urge neutrality upon you, while he who is your ally will urge you to take sides." Yet, because war is inevitable, a policy of neutrality, he believed, would ultimately be disastrous, and those who adopt such a policy "usually destroy themselves by doing so."

In regard to the second justification, Machiavelli advises, "because you cannot always win if you respect the rules, you must be prepared to break them." It's interesting to see how such a no-holds-barred policy may sound delightfully savage when its aim is directed at others; however, when it's directed at the very citizens being served and protected by the government, for example, regarding invasions of privacy, evidently citizens don't find it so delightful.

Finally, Machiavelli's comments on the humanitarian policy of compassion apply to both justifications for Dirty Hands. Machiavelli warned rulers to be careful about being compassionate, for, on the one hand, it's more compassionate to be harsh with a few than to permit disorder and lawlessness to spread. On the other hand, Machiavelli explains that you should *seem* to be compassionate and trustworthy, sympathetic and honest, while at the same time fully prepared, if they become liabilities, to "become their opposites." Thus, in a perhaps uncomfortable summation, Machiavelli advises, "Whenever you have to kill someone, make sure you have a suitable excuse."

It's for Your Own Good!

But, why must government appear to have "clean hands" at all? If you're a tyrant or a despot, then having clean hands may be of little consequence. However, the reason a democratic government, such as the one governing the United States of America, would need to appear to have clean hands is that their actions (by definition in a democracy) are supposed to be acceptable to the public. In other words, not just the *ends* but also the *means* of government action are supposed to be susceptible to public scrutiny and influence.

As a result, checks and balances such as transparency and accountability are considered necessary for a democratic society. And yet, these checks and balances may be seen as detrimental, from a Machiavellian point of view, to the best interests of the citizens who are being governed, unless, of course, the primary interest of the citizens is to remain within a true democracy.

So, how might these ideas from Machiavelli relate to WikiLeaks? Given the massive amount of information leaked to the public by WikiLeaks, we will only look at the greatest leaks, or what have also been called their greatest revelations or biggest secrets revealed as of September 2017. Using such terms to search the Internet the following leaks consistently appear (though not necessarily in the following order): 1. Climate change falsification in one of the most prestigious and supposedly professionally peer-reviewed academic journals of science; 2. What is being called the "killing of innocents"; 3. Loss of privacy regarding domestic CIA spying tactics; 4. US-Israel funding of ISIS, specifically, and the popular conspiracy theory of involvement in 9/11 by officials of the American government, generally. Again, this list is based on what would appear for anyone searching the Internet with such terms as "biggest WikiLeaks" and so on.

Before addressing each of these leaks from a Machiavellian point of view, from the perspective of the history of Western philosophy, WikiLeaks is basically just providing evidence for what many philosophers, especially contemporary French philosophers such as Jean-Paul Sartre, Gilles Deleuze, and Jean Baudrillard have been suggesting in regard to the global "War Machine" since the late 1960s and 1970s.

These French philosophers are critical of capitalism and its role, discussed in terms of tax dollars and shopping sprees, in circulating capital, or loosely put money, to fuel the "War Machine." Put more directly, when you make that purchase your participation in the capitalist market helps to pay for the weapons used "to kill our enemies" or, put more patriotically, "in the defense of our nation." In fact, the name of this dilemma, "The Problem of Dirty Hands," comes from Sartre's play of the same name.

The issue is that despite the glaring tensions between the principles of democracy and purposefully misinforming citizens, as per the Machiavelli political strategy playbook, it may not be immediately clear in regard to all the issues that some of the subterfuge *isn't* in the best interest of a nation's citizens. According to a kind of unashamed Machiavellianism, the "War Machine," for lack of a better word, is *good*, precisely because it defends our nation by killing our enemies. What's more, keeping in mind that Machiavelli wrote in the sixteenth century, it may be the case that this type of scenario, between the morality of citizens and the immorality of governments, is part of the very nature of the activity of governing humans. An exemplar case, invoked by the movie *Imitation Game* (2014), and not involving the United States government, was the "Coventry Blitz," in which the utilitarian decision was made not to evacuate the English city of Coventry, despite knowing that it would be bombed, because doing so would have revealed that the British had cracked the code the Germans were using to communicate military objectives.

Lies, Damned Lies, and Statistics

Specifically, then, with regard to the falsification of climate change data published in *Nature*, academics since the leak have been scrambling to suggest that the emails don't say what they appear to say. However, the statistical "trick," as the scientists themselves referred to it, used to promulgate misinformation illustrates what some theorists have long been suggesting in regard to the elite, academic or otherwise, and their capacity to control, or at least influence, the masses through misinformation.

This WikiLeak, then, illustrates, at the least, how academic honesty and professional peer-review may, in some instances, be considered mere lip service for what's ultimately behind propaganda generated and promulgated in support of various political agendas.

With regard to "the killing of innocents," WikiLeaks posted video footage from the gunsight of a US Apache helicopter, calling the video "Collateral Murder," in Baghdad in July, 2007. Of course, as Machiavelli may have characterized it, the fact that your soldiers are prone to violence and celebrate violence should be considered good. For instance, if you were to need a bodyguard, you would probably want someone who not only knows how to fight but also is looking for potential threats, rather than someone engaged in too much of an internal conflict to be able to defend you, with the "celebrations" that keep them primed for violence intended to be kept private. Moreover, Machiavelli wouldn't seem to have a problem with such "collateral murder," though he would advocate for a good excuse afterward, perhaps one promulgated through a professionally peer-reviewed academic journal.

Domestic spying by the CIA and the issue of the loss of privacy appeared recently in *Social Epistemology and Technology* (2015) and the Fourth Special Issue of the *Social Epistemology Review and Reply Collective* (social-epistemology.com). Before the WikiLeaks release, the suggestion that the CIA might be spying on Americans through their smartphones or smart TVs may have seemed a product of paranoia or dismissed as a conspiracy theory. However, now that WikiLeaks has provided confirmation of exactly such means through which domestic surveillance occurs, there's concern regarding the loss of privacy.

Yet, again, as we noticed above, Machiavelli warned against too much compassion, as if advocating *for* domestic surveillance as an appropriate means against "allowing disorder to spread." In other words, if your neighbor is plotting to blow you up, you might want the government to intervene before it happens. However, how can the government know about your nefarious neighbor if it respects the rules of privacy?

Lastly, with regard to the relationship between the US-Israeli "military-industrial complex" and ISIS, it's neither clear from the leaks nor from the commentators regarding the leaks just what has been revealed. The two main theses regarding which commentators seem to be searching the leaks are, first, that ISIS is funded by the US and Israel and, second, that 9/11 was an "inside job." Speculation seems to be based on a wide range of data, for example, from leaked emails to the fact that ISIS seems to have a fleet of matching Toyota trucks.

Yet, again, as heart-wrenching as it certainly will be for some to hear, suppose these theses were true. They would be consistent with a Machiavellian style of statecraft. In other words, Machiavelli would advocate for the subterfuge resulting in the appearance of "clean hands" by fabricating an enemy so as to justify military intervention to the citizens for reasons other than the actual political reasons. And, as we've seen already, the fact that innocent people would lose their lives in a government staging of such subterfuge wouldn't be a deterrent for Machiavelli.

You Can't Handle the Truth!

What's at stake from a Machiavellian point of view regarding WikiLeaks? On the one hand, it's reasonable to acknowledge how a policy of neutrality and compassion in the face of domestic terror isn't ideal. On the other hand, it's equally reasonable to acknowledge how a policy of transparency may be a necessary condition for citizens truly to participate in a democracy. This may even be the case if we acknowledge scarcity of resources and the inevitability of war. For example, this is why Noam Chomsky refers to the impetus behind WikiLeaks as "taking citizenship seriously." Yet, at the same time, especially if WMDs aren't simply a "good excuse" for invasion, isn't a no-holds-barred approach to defense ideal?

These questions must resound as rhetorical, since citizens, even with the knowledge leaked by WikiLeaks, seem incapable of democratically changing the global situation in which we now find ourselves. Seen in the light of the tension between the principles of democracy and the principles of Machiavellian statecraft, these issues raised by revelations from WikiLeaks aren't easily resolved.

Recall the "Coventry Blitz" dilemma, and we may further note the idea that the government may make decisions deemed in the best interest of its citizens, despite the fact that those decisions lead directly to the deaths of many of its own innocents, has probably been a moral dilemma tested more times in Western history than citizens realize.

Yet, at the same time, if citizens could know, is it *good* for them to know? Do they really *need* to know? Perhaps not too unlike an unexpected pregnancy, then, citizens may want to know the truth of the situations in which they participate, thereby embracing WikiLeaks and its revelations. Or, perhaps it's the case, as Machiavelli and Colonel Jessup from *A Few Good Men* (1992) might suggest, if you are a citizen: "You can't handle the truth!"

9
Information Wants to Be True?

CHRISTOPHER KETCHAM

Physicists want us to believe that information never disappears. However, Stephen Hawking proposed that information *could* be lost in black holes. But Leonard Susskind has fought back with the idea that information remains around the black hole's event horizon.

This suggests that if we had the tools, and the time, we could reconstruct the information that's been shredded by the cosmic black hole. We could also say that everything you've ever said and thought might also *never* disappear. Gone missing, perhaps, but never *gone* gone. Frightening thought.

All the Information?

WikiLeaks information, disseminated to news agencies and the public, also never disappears. Let's be clear, though: *WikiLeaks is a conduit, both a receptacle and a fount for information.* What we must confront is the question of the possibility of information that WikiLeaks *misses*, what they never get or never release.

Here's the question: *If we know that WikiLeaks may not get complete information or may withhold information they receive, and that information is often redacted by third parties before it's released to the public, then how do we make informed decisions about what is true, partially true, or not at all true?*

As we observe the world and process phenomena in our minds, we gain information. Before humans could read and write, observation and language were how we gained that information. Primitive mythologies came from the observations of the world around us. These mythologies may have had some basis in observed or experienced phenomena, but their basis in *fact* has long since become suspect with the rise of the scientific method.

We read fiction and believe it and enjoy it for what it is— make-believe. We read about information in the form of textbooks and scientific journals and call them facts, with the caveat that these facts can change when new information is provided. We realize that history books don't chronicle the actual events as they occurred. History is composed from hermeneutic, or interpretive, data associated with personal accounts, news accounts, embedded photographers, official documents, analysis of other interpretations of the same history, and the project of the author of the particular accounts. After further analysis, we realize that in some volume of World War II history, there are no interviews with people from the war's losing side or neutral side, only the winners. How much truth is in a "true" account where only one side of the conflict is represented?

What if the WikiLeaks donor, leaker, or informant only gives you what they want you to know? What if their agenda isn't to release information to make it free but to do irreparable damage by releasing altered or selective information so that readers draw only the donor's conclusion from the information they receive? The donor knows this will cause damage because the secret agency from which it was taken won't, or can't, divulge that information has been taken and, therefore, doesn't weigh in on whether the information is complete or incomplete, authentic or inauthentic.

History isn't some static object we call "true." It's an evolving interpretation much like science, looking ever deeper into phenomena to gain knowledge from what they show us. We must have sufficient and authentic data to make truth claims about the phenomena being studied. To call something "true" in the absolute sense, we would need *all* the information related to it. This would include information from our senses, and even those we can't sense, such as infrared and ultraviolet light. We would need to know the effects the phenomenon has on things like atomic structure and other objects in the universe. So much information would come at us that we would have great difficulty determining what it is that we are saying is "true."

How Much Truth?

We can approach information and truth claims in two ways. First, the truth claim is true unless proven otherwise. The spectrum of "otherwise than true" can run from just more than completely false to just less than completely true. We can't get to either completely true or completely false because information *is* information, and just by observing, it changes. So, we can never get to the absolute truth of the matter. Therefore, we can say that information *is*, but is never absolutely true or false.

Information exists even when it's compiled, sorted, extracted, and used to convert information into truth claims. When it's analyzed as a thing in itself, or it's combined with other data, the analysis and interpretation of information results in truth claims that are subject to further analysis on the truth spectrum.

Point to an object and offer the truth claim "That's a rock." It may be, but unless you further analyze the object, you may not discover that it's actually a piece of plastic that looks like a rock or a bit of petrified bone that's taken on a rock-like form. "She's blonde" is one of the more problematic truth claims. She may have dyed her hair or the blondeness is such that one might also call it dirty blonde or even brunette with streaks of blonde. Let's modify the truth claim to say "She's an actress who always appears platinum blonde in the movies and in public." Can we say, then, for purposes of assigning her the label "blonde," that she's blonde? We accept the statement as "true" until the paparazzi snaps a picture of her out in public that shows otherwise.

The other approach sees the truth claim as being "false" until shown otherwise. We can use either approach depending on the source of the material and the familiarity, if any, we have with the information that's being supplied. For example, you have confidence that a particular news service has provided you with good information in the past, so you're willing to assume that its "truth" claims are accurate . . . unless proven otherwise. However, a different news service often enough serves up spectacularly speculative truth claims, for example, about Hollywood starlets having alien babies. You're likely to treat such "truths" as being false until proven otherwise.

Which Truth?

How did you get to where you trusted the one's "truths" and not the other's? Critical thinking. However, critical thinking isn't easily defined. Tim Moore looked at seven different definitions of critical thinking and found seven "definitional strands" in the disciplines of history, philosophy, and cultural studies. These aren't disciplines with mathematical proofs or rigid scientific method protocol experiments that can be statistically evaluated and replicated.

The disciplines of history, philosophy, and cultural studies involve human activity, logic, and understanding—a much messier business. The definitional terms Moore found are: judgment, skepticism, simple originality, sensitive reading, rationality, activist engagement with knowledge, and self-reflexivity.

We might use all or just a few of these to first determine whether to consider the first news outlet as generally more truthful than the second news outlet. Even if we choose not to read articles from the second outlet, when we read an article from the first, we will likely also use some or all of these critical thinking processes to determine for ourselves whether or not we find the information presented consistent with our own opinion of the news outlet. We then may conduct research outside of that article to see what others say, which begins the critical thinking process anew. How exhausting. But, this isn't the end of it.

Philosopher R.G. Collingwood (1889–1943) said, "Every statement that anyone ever makes is made in answer to a question." Collingwood proposed that we exist in an infinite loop of questions that produce statements that produce further questions, and so on. However, we must begin somewhere, put our stake in the ground with a first question. In the case of WikiLeaks, that question is whether we begin any encounter with WikiLeaks information from the position of "true unless proven otherwise" or "false unless proven otherwise."

To begin to answer that question, we need to ask questions about the WikiLeaks organization, its sources of information, its human face, and how it operates. Because WikiLeaks operates in the clandestine world of state secrets and intelligence, don't be disappointed if we find no definitive answers, only more questions. However, this process can nevertheless help us determine whether following WikiLeaks and the news outlets that analyze and publish WikiLeaks data are places we might turn to for access to the truth. Along the way, use your own judgement, skepticism, simple originality, sensitive reading, rationality, activist engagement with knowledge, and self-reflexivity on the material presented. In other words, do your own critical thinking, and critique what *I'm* presenting as "facts" or "truth."

Wiki-Truths

First, WikiLeaks is a not-for-profit organization. Ah, we say, that's a good sign because not-for-profit organizations don't have the conflict of interest of maximizing profits for their shareholders. However, there have been many instances where not-for-profits have acted like for-profit entities because of the exorbitant salary and benefits they pay to founders and officers. Not-for-profit status is no sure indicator that WikiLeaks will provide information from which we can assemble truth claims.

Second, WikiLeaks prides itself on its ability to provide anonymity and its strong encryption and other protective devices that help keep "free" information captive within its servers until it's ready to release that information. WikiLeaks has a conduit and has a reservoir of data it hasn't yet shared, and we can't know if they'll ever share it. WikiLeaks accepts anonymous donations of information. Anonymity certainly can help shield the donor from the law or from discovery by the target organization and others. There's a reason why the donor has given the information to WikiLeaks. That motivation may have colored the type of information that the donor supplies.

If the donor has a strong agenda or ideological stance and good knowledge about how the information is generated by the organization, what's to prevent the donor from creating *new* information that will help boost the donor's agenda or cause? If information that the donor supplies comes from clandestine organizations, such as the CIA or Interpol, these organizations may not ever acknowledge that this information was generated from their work. However, there may be anonymous knowledgeable sources that come forward and suggest that, "Yes, this came from the archives of X, or yes, this is produced in the style of Y, or, this looks like it could have come from Z." Then again, even the 'non-ideological' donor (fat chance) may only have access to certain information. What the donor hasn't had access to might be more important. We will never know.

What we have is a chain of anonymity involving the anonymous WikiLeaks, the anonymous donor, and the anonymous "knowledgeable" source who offers that the source of the information likely comes from where the donor says it does. This chain of anonymity certainly doesn't give us the highest level of confidence that the information was generated by the organization in question or that there's information from the same source that has already countermanded the released information or would otherwise shade the released information in a different light. We're left in a kind of no-man's-land of confidence intervals subject to extreme swings as information is investigated and more anonymous leakers, anonymous informants, and anonymous (or not anonymous) 'experts' analyze the data to confirm its 'probable' source and authenticity . . . or not.

Suppose the CIA director explains that these leaks represent a breach of national security, and the CIA arrests, tries, convicts, and sentences to prison for a very long time a mole within the organization who released the documents. Both actions only inform us that at least some of the information probably came from the CIA. But how much? Most of it, some of it, or just a little bit of it? We're handicapped up front with attributing truth claims associated with the possibilities that WikiLeaks has obtained limited information, information that may have been created in-part by the donor to bolster the donor's agenda, or is mixed in with information sources not associated with the target that may be used simply to make the pile of information appear larger and more substantial.

We might become immediately suspicious of the latter if information includes e-mail exchanges between organiza-tion employees sharing recipes . . . unless, of course, the (anonymous or otherwise) "knowledgeable" analysts suggest that a recipe is in fact an encoded hidden message that deals directly with the activities of the organization that the donor has determined need to see the light of day.

Doesn't WikiLeaks content go directly from the donor through the servers and into the public domain? Not exactly. WikiLeaks operators, employees or otherwise—we can't be sure—first assess the information to make sure it isn't otherwise available, speculative, or clouded in mystery as to its source. Next, is it interesting to WikiLeaks's audience, and more importantly, will it enhance the image of WikiLeaks in the eyes of the reader and others who see it as being a champion of information freedom?

Rather than dump the load of thousands upon thousands of obtained information pieces and messages, WikiLeaks operatives hoard the information and release it at opportune times to keep the WikiLeaks name con-tinuously in the public eye. This wasn't always the case. In the beginning, WikiLeaks released data directly to the public. As WikiLeaks became inundated with data, they began to hoard it and then send small batches to select news organizations who redact information that might get the news organization in trouble or might "out" innocent parties.

Then, sifting through the narrow slice of the incomplete information package that was sent, as good investigative journalists are trained to do, the news organizations provide a hermeneutic explanation (like the historians) of the data, giving their own journalistic "truth" claims to what their investigations have discovered. This is what we expect journalists and historians to do, distill and summarize, and then give their theories about what happened in the form of "truth" claims. This saves us a lot of time, and if the news organizations are those we believe are generally credible, we might accept that what we read in the news is the "truth."

What WikiLeaks and we have done is to give over to others, albeit well trained, seasoned, and, by nature skeptical, journalists the task of sifting through all that data. What if some of what they included in their analysis is donor-created data? What if the data the donor provided is authentic, but is only data that the donor believes supports the donor's agenda for supplying it, and missing data would lead to an entirely different interpretation? What if WikiLeaks is selectively sending data to the news organization to pursue their own agenda? What if the news organization is known to have systematic biases towards or against the organization from which the data has been leaked? "'Truth" is only as good as the information that's available to back up the statement.

Remember the *Maine*!

Go back in time. The Battleship *Maine* blew up in Havana Harbor in 1898, coincidentally while the Cubans were revolting against their colonial masters in Spain. After much investigation at the time and subsequent refutations and challenges to the findings that an external mine destroyed the *Maine*, we still do not have *the* reason the *Maine* suddenly blew up. Newspapermen Joseph Pulitzer and William Randolph Hearst played up the external mine theory to the point where they swayed public opinion towards the US intervening. Teddy Roosevelt charged up San Juan Hill with his Rough Riders to national fame.

In 1901, Roosevelt, who had been elected William McKinley's Vice President, succeeded McKinley when he was assassinated. The succession of "truth" claims pushed by the press not only released Cuba from Spanish control, but changed the course of history by making Theodore Roosevelt a household name and hero who parlayed this into the presidency. What's scarier than a blown-up battleship is the other-than-complete or authentic information people believe that ultimately leads to war in the age of nuclear weapons. Therefore, the importance of "truth" claims and the information behind them can't be overstated.

Thar's Gold in Them Thar Data

So far, we have anonymous data, donors, and analysis within WikiLeaks itself. We have the parceling out of data by anonymous WikiLeaks operatives to select news organizations who further redact the material and reduce it to journalistic analysis and 'sound-bites' which serve as "truth" claims. We can also say that it's a boost to "truth" when multiple news organizations do their own independent research from the WikiLeaks parceled-out data and come up with quite similar conclusions and "sound-bites."

What WikiLeaks and the journalists want us to believe is that they get raw rock from the stream, crush it, then pan it for the flakes of gold that result. The gold represents the "truth." The other information is just debris that doesn't relate to the original search for gold. How much of the rocks that were supplied by the donor and WikiLeaks were designed to produce the end-product of "golden truth," when in fact the more important story was that there was also titanium in the mix further upstream that would ultimately become a much more important find? Titanium isn't discovered because the information that indicated that it's present is never provided. We may never know whether WikiLeaks chose not to release the information about the rocks that were discovered upstream or if the donor never gave WikiLeaks that information, caring only that the 'golden truth' be the one that journalists and researchers derive from the data. *If all they ever serve you is chicken necks, you'll never discover the more tender and perhaps tastier chicken breast.*

What About Assange?

Finally, we must at least question the credibility of the spokesperson and one of the founders of WikiLeaks, Julian Assange, who took sanctuary in the Ecuadorian embassy in London to avoid extradition to Sweden on charges of alleged sexual improprieties (charges which have since been dropped). That's not the least of his worries, because those countries whose secrets WikiLeaks has allegedly outed want him for questioning. Whether the allegations of sexual impropriety are true, exaggerated by authorities to provide a means of arresting Assange where other efforts have failed, or are entirely false, we must ask the question of whether this is someone from whom we can expect fair dealings. That said, we can also explain away his legal troubles by calling him a martyr for freedom of information, even if it's so-called government secrets.

The problem, then, is this. Whenever there is one person, and only one person, who is the spokesperson and contact for the organization, that person's credibility and character is all that we have to assess whether the information being disseminated is authentic, skewed towards an agenda, or inauthentic. Since the rest of the

WikiLeaks organization has remained in the shadows, Assange is what we have to represent the human part of the WikiLeaks equation. Do you trust that Julian Assange is giving you authentic information?

So What's It Going to Be?

We're back at the beginning with as many questions and not so many answers. All that WikiLeaks gets, stores, and disseminates is information. Of that we can be certain. Whether the information is authentic or complete, we can't be sure. Agencies from whom classified information is stolen may not reveal the completeness or accuracy of the information in any meaningful way. The most we might get from these agencies is that it's "damaging to national security." Next, we don't know the motivations behind the leakers themselves, and therefore we don't know whether or when we might be getting incomplete information that helps the leaker's agenda. We may not ever know whether the information released can produce a complete picture of events, distorts events, or has been determined to be "false" through other information that was not leaked . . . or released by WikiLeaks. Finally, we have Assange, the sole spokesperson for the secretive secret-outing not-for-profit who's wanted by the world for various alleged infractions and who speaks as a refugee from the Ecuadorian Embassy in London.

Sure, we want information to be true. We want to trust people who have given us good and authentic information and made informed "truth" claims. However, WikiLeaks information requires additional levels of scrutiny which we hope that news services and other analysts of the leaked information have been doing their due diligence to authenticate. Even then, we must worry that WikiLeaks is withholding much of the information it's received to parcel it out at a later date to keep its name in the public eye, or for other purposes of which we aren't aware. We don't know whether, when the next batch of leaks is released, many of the "truth" claims that journalists and others will derive from the information will have to be changed or refuted when WikiLeaks releases its next batch of cables. We wonder also whether unnecessary damage has been caused by the selective release of information. We may believe the idea with WikiLeaks that information shouldn't be sequestered by governments, that it should be allowed to be free. However, by hoarding data and having others redact that data, what degrees of this promised freedom are being abrogated by actions bent on serving WikiLeaks and the news agencies to whom they distribute?

To get closer to the truth, all information must be free, not just selective parts, perhaps not even just relevant parts—because, who decides relevancy? Therefore, for WikiLeaks information and the resulting 'truth' claims that are derived from this information, I put a question mark after making the statement, "Information wants to be true?" This suggests that one must continue to use critical thinking—judgement, skepticism, simple originality, sensitive reading, rationality, activist engagement with knowledge, and self-reflexivity whenever one encounters WikiLeaks 'truths'.

Back to the original question. How will you treat WikiLeaks now—as "true unless proven otherwise" or as "false unless proven otherwise"?

Fifth Dump

Fake News

10
On WikiLeaks and Bullshit

MARLENE CLARK

> WikiLeaks is a giant library of the world's most persecuted documents. We give asylum to these documents, we analyze them, we promote them and we obtain more.
>
> —JULIAN ASSANGE, *Der Spiegel* interview

I call bullshit.

So did Emmanuel Macron, when, two days before the French run-off election of May 7th 2017, WikiLeaks, in a precisely timed *attaque de feinte*, announced a forthcoming dump of emails and documents from the Macron campaign.

To be precise, neither 4Chan nor WikiLeaks—both of whom first were assigned credit or blame (take your pick) by reputable media outlets, including NPR—published the Friday night dump, according to an *emptywheel* article entitled "Why Accuracy about WikiLeaks Matters." But both posted links to the Pastebin containing the cache, and both widely publicized the leak on Facebook and Twitter, with links to the documents themselves. Bots took over and quickly moved the news from France to the United States.

All of this occurred at the proverbial eleventh hour, quite literally. Officially, the French campaign ended at midnight on Friday, May 5th, when the "curtain of silence" fell as the French began casting their weekend ballots. The promised dump occurred just a couple of hours before midnight. And so, with just over a hundred minutes to respond, the Macron campaign issued a poorly edited bombshell announcement: Some of the documents in the cache were fakes. Alert and wary after the steady drip, drip, drip of the Podesta and DNC leaks had so damaged the credibility of the Clinton campaign in the United States, Macron and his campaign claimed they had anticipated a similar "asylum" of their "persecuted documents," and rendered them moot by larding them with bullshit.

WikiLeaks quickly answered the *retraite de feint* by claiming that though they hadn't as yet completely vetted the documents for authenticity (and hence not published), they had thus far found no fakes in #MacronLeaks. Moreover, they countered with the claim that they were "skeptical that the Macron campaign is faster than us." The claim of superior speed is curious, since the Macron campaign statement insinuated it had been posting phony emails and documents, designed to deceive should the need arise, throughout the course of campaign, and not just in the past couple days once they were warned. It was WikiLeaks, rather, that was under the gun to verify everything in time to publish before the election.

That WikiLeaks posted an announcement and a link to elsewhere, rather than the dump itself, showed only that it had busted its own deadline, and nothing more. So, a more accurate wording to express WikiLeaks's pique may have been, perhaps, "We are skeptical that the Macron campaign is *smarter* than us."

The election ended on Sunday, May 7th, with a decisive victory for Macron.

Is It Really Bullshit?

Few of us hesitate to say, "Oh bullshit!" or "That's bullshit!" whether in anger or jest without giving much thought as to what "bullshit" actually may be. The philosopher Harry G. Frankfurt, thankfully, isn't one of those people. His careful, only slightly tongue-in-cheek, Montaigne-like study, *On Bullshit*, attempts to get at the "structure of the concept" of bullshit.

His brief book does an admirable job, though it's at times difficult to distinguish bullshit from the bullshitter—a pitfall to be expected, I suppose, since every emission requires an emitter. Relying on Frankfurt's analysis, let's examine the purportedly corrupt #MacronLeaks and the man ultimately behind them, Emmanuel Macron. Frankfurt's path leads us mostly through a thicket of questions: If there really are fake documents and emails embedded in the #MacronLeaks dump, are they bullshit? If Macron orchestrated their inclusion, is he a bullshitter? Suppose, alternatively, that there are no phony documents and emails: is Macron's claim that there are simply bullshit? And does the doubt the claim inserts, either way, make #MacronLeaks—and, by extension, this dump of WikiLeaks—bullshit in any event?

Connecting bullshit to one of its more benign *Oxford English Dictionary* synonyms, "humbug," doesn't get Frankfurt where he wants to go, but his ride gains some traction when he turns to the ever-reliable GPS of language usage, Ludwig Wittgenstein, for guidance. In due course, Frankfurt isolates bullshit's many salient characteristics.

First, bullshit is carefully wrought. As Frankfurt immediately sees, this claim at least at first seems to be out of place. Bullshit is excrement, and who among us painstakingly crafts bodily emissions? Yet Frankfurt begs to differ and points, aptly, to politics as an example "replete with instances of bullshit" and "exquisitely sophisticated craftsmen who dedicate themselves tirelessly to getting every word and image they produce exactly right."

Macron, no different from others in his field, crafted his political image just so. Hence, he was unwilling to have that image disrupted or possibly annihilated by emails and documents revealing him to be other than the near-perfect specimen he projected to the French people. Moreover, if there were false emails and documents added to his files, they too were likely carefully created to appear "real" and pass WikiLeaks's scrutiny.

Second, bullshit entails laxity. This, too, at first appears counterintuitive. Nothing about the first criterion would suggest laxity or carelessness; in fact, one would expect laxity to result in sloppiness. And yet, the inclusion of false documents indicates a less than faithful rendering of the truth, which is a form of laxity or irresponsibility. In Macron's case, this form of laxity could be considered a case of ends justifying the means or, to put it in other words, a responsible form of irresponsibility. He thought himself the best candidate for the job, in every way superior to and better for France than the far-right candidate, Marine Le Pen. Nevertheless, his unconcern for truth in this instance, this indifference to how things really are, in his emails, which Macron's gambit seems to embrace, is the very essence of bullshit, according to Frankfurt.

Third, bullshit isn't "for real." Frankfurt connects the "not real" here with "hot air." Hot air, when associated with speech, is merely "vapor" leaving the speaker's mouth, "without substance or content." Notably, hot air, according to Frankfurt, offers up "an especially suitable equivalent for bullshit." Both are voided bodily waste; bullshit, like all excrement, emptied of "nutritive" content, hot air empty of "informative" content.

Though #MacronLeaks "speak" through writing rather than speech, Frankfurt's point still holds true. Not only are the phony emails and documents "hot air" and empty of "real" content, but you could argue that their inclusion turns the entire dump into cotton candy, spun sugar that immediately dissolves on the tongue, its trace exhaled as a sweet hot vapor, empty of nutritional value to political junkies and disrupters alike.

Fourth, bullshit is closer to a bluff than a lie. The French electorate and, we hope, *any* electorate, would be appalled to learn they had elected a liar. But a bluff is not a lie. Lies deliberately misrepresent the truth; bluffs blow smoke. According to Frankfurt, lies imply falsity, while bluffs suggest "fakery," an important distinction. Bullshit, like Macron's fabricated documents and emails, entails phoniness, not mendacity. And here Frankfurt makes an important point for our case: "one must need recognize that a fake or phony need not be in any respect (apart from authenticity) inferior to the real thing." In fact, what is "not genuine" must be an "exact copy" of the "real thing."

This observation returns us to the idea that bullshit is carefully wrought. If #MacronLeaks was to lead WikiLeaks down the garden path of error and embarrassment, the fake must be an exact copy of the real to pull off the deception. What's more, the "fake" material included in #MacronLeaks need not necessarily be false statements, just, perhaps, not accurate in their context. And so, Frankfurt avers that we "presume not only that there is an important difference between lying and bullshit, but that the latter is preferable to the former."

Frankfurt's distinction here well serves Macron. He isn't guilty of lies, which could be politically treacherous, but rather of bullshitting, which is quite all right, even enviable in certain circumstances, especially this one. Moreover, in this case, the bullshit was *advertised*; Macron's challenge to WikiLeaks wasn't covert but public. And the French responded with a typically Gallic shrug of nonchalance. They understood that Macron was bullshitting Julian Assange and WikiLeaks, not them.

Fifth, bullshit "misrepresents neither the state of affairs to which it refers nor the beliefs of the speaker concerning the state of affairs." These two criteria clearly apply to Macron's case. He announced publicly that the false as well as the true were embedded in his campaign documents, and hence they couldn't be taken as a reflection of his beliefs during the campaign. But he wasn't so much seeking to deceive the French people about his own enterprise as he was hoping to expose the potential falsity in WikiLeaks's agenda, in that it claims to aim to bring truth to light when in reality it seems (at least recently) that it hopes to tilt elections to far-right candidates.

Sixth, the bullshitter doesn't want to lie; he just wants to "attain a goal." Clearly, Macron's intent wasn't to lie, but to get elected.

Seventh, bullshitting tends to make the bullshitter unfit for the truth. Certainly, habitual bullshitting, "creative hyperbole," or the constant citing of "alternative facts" will eventually cloud even the bullshitter's judgment as to what's true and what's bullshit. But the people of France understood that this case was a one-off. No one read Macron as a chronic bullshitter; in fact, he represented himself, and seemed to be accepted, as a straight shooter. Especially since in this case, he admitted his fabrications as a means to outsmarting Assange and his enterprise.

Eighth, bullshitters are smart. They stop short of lying. The Macron campaign—and by extension Macron himself as its spokesperson—cleverly sought to deceive Assange and WikiLeaks about what was on its mind, without lying. Since no one could know for sure which emails and documents were genuine and which were fake, and since Macron publicly proclaimed the strategy, his announcement not only stops short of the outright lie, it trumpets truth.

Macron also looks very smart. No candidate or campaign before had thought of using Macron's gambit. But then again, Macron's campaign followed shortly after Hillary Clinton and the Clinton campaign experienced the ramifications of the chaos sown by campaign leaks exposed to a public lately weary of politics as usual.

Macron and his campaign decided they needed to outwit WikiLeaks to avoid similar exposure and its damaging consequences. With just hours left before the election, there was no time to lose to bombshell revelations and their fallout. The threatened dump had to be neutralized quickly and efficiently, and it was. WikiLeaks—and by extension Julian Assange—need not be skeptical. Macron and his campaign were smart enough to temporarily thwart WikiLeaks and Assange when it really mattered. In other words, Macron successfully bullshitted them.

WikiLeaks finally published what David Leonhardt has called the "spectacularly mundane" Macron campaign email dump on July 31st 2017. It sincerely and steadfastly claimed all had been carefully vetted and authenticated. This claim leaves Macron's assertion an open question. Perhaps Macron's statement of May 5th 2017 was, in and of itself, bullshit. Then again, maybe some "authenticated" emails, thanks to all their cleverness, careful craft, and "truthiness," passed as real when in fact they were bullshit. If in fact that's the case, we can conclude, according to the criteria laid out by Frankfurt, that at least in this one instance what WikiLeaks published is in part bullshit, and Monsieur Macron is a sometime bullshitter. Both Macron and his campaign and Assange and WikiLeaks claim the high road of sincerity.

But as Frankfurt concludes: Sincerity itself? *C'est des conneries.*

11
Bad Faith and WikiLeaks

KIMBERLY S. ENGELS

Since the first leaks were released in 2007, almost everyone has formed an opinion of the website WikiLeaks and its founder Julian Assange. Whether WikiLeaks leaks information that supports or challenges our beliefs has much to do with whether we view them favorably or not. WikiLeaks has become a controversial, often inconvenient, omnipresent fact of the modern moral landscape.

The provocative website releases high-value information related to corruption in the government, corporations, political parties, militaries, and war. The threat that our actions can be anonymously reported and then exposed to the public poses a new set of conditions through which powerful people experience the modern world.

Sartrean Insights

Jean-Paul Sartre (1905–1980), a twentieth-century philosopher famous for his views on human freedom and responsibility, argued that each person builds his or her essence through a choice of themselves in the world. Because humans are free, we're also responsible both for our actions and who we choose to be. However, we tend to avoid this responsibility by lying to ourselves. Sartre called this act "bad faith." If we examine WikiLeaks through a Sartrean lens, we can show how WikiLeaks introduces an altered field of possibilities for powerful individuals who engage in corrupt behavior and how it forces some of these same individuals to accept the strong sense of responsibility that Sartre argues is necessary for remaining outside of bad faith.

WikiLeaks uses modern technology to allow people to submit information anonymously, and then the information is released to the public online. This anonymous online format makes WikiLeaks appear impersonal or robotic, but WikiLeaks is ultimately simply about the behavior of individual human beings. It is human beings who engage in corrupt behavior, human beings who deliver classified information to the WikiLeaks site, and human beings who release the information to the public.

I will refer to individuals who may be exposed by WikiLeaks as "powerful individuals," and this term is meant to encompass people working for governments, corporations, political parties, or any other organization that has significant influence over citizens' lives and who have the ability to manipulate, control, and harm the public. Moreover, these individuals have access to the resources necessary both to support and to cover up their behavior. As WikiLeaks is ultimately about the choices of human beings, it makes sense to examine WikiLeaks through the lens of a philosopher who wrote extensively on what it meant to be an individual who makes choices in the world.

Freedom and Responsibility

Sartre is most famous for his views on freedom, but his theory of freedom has to be understood as part of his overall view of human experience. Sartre argued that each human being is free to choose oneself in the world through a "project." We build ourselves in the world by projecting ourselves towards a future that we hope to be, but aren't yet. Thus, our "essences," or core selves, are malleable and not fixed or permanent. At any time we are free to make a new choice of ourselves in the world.

My existential project as a philosophy professor means I organize my behavior around certain objectives: to teach students and to write research. My "project" is the collection of choices I make that, when viewed as a whole, comprise my essence, my core self. However, just as I am free at any time to choose no longer to be a philosophy professor, so we all are free at any time to choose a new project and change our essence. This is what lies behind Sartre's argument that "existence precedes essence." It is through living, or existing in a certain way, that we form our essence.

Our choice of project or self, however, doesn't occur in a vacuum. We build that essence against an array of social and material conditions or constraints. We also can't make a choice of self that transcends our "facticity," those characteristics about ourselves that we can't change, such as our biological sex, our race, our ethnicity, or the socio-economic class into which we're born. Therefore, while I may be free to quit my job as a philosophy professor and apply for a job at the local deli, I'm not free to quit my job and become the King of England. My facticity and situation place limits on my freedom and my project.

We make our existential choices within a web of relationships with other people whom Sartre refers to as "Others." When we experience the world by ourselves, we freely interpret it as a world that's there for us. But, when another person enters the picture, we realize that an environment that was previously there only for us is also there for them. We also realize that our actions become subject to interpretation by another free human being, an Other. This feeling of being *watched* changes our own interpretation of our situation. This is part of what Sartre means by his famous line that "Hell is other people"—the introduction of another person whose freedom we can't control places limits on our own freedom and changes our perception of ourselves. We're no longer as free as we once were.

Don't Lie to Me!

Sartre wrote extensively on the issue of bad faith, that is to say, *lying to ourselves*. Sartre says that bad faith arises when we either deny our freedom to choose or deny our facticity. He uses the example of a waiter in a café. In some sense, he *is* a waiter, because that's part of his project. It's a role he plays and a choice he's made. If he says "I'm not a waiter," then he would be in bad faith. Simultaneously, if he denies that being a waiter is a free choice that he makes, that's also a form of bad faith. Moreover, he has to acknowledge the constraints that might lead him to keep the job—quitting his post as a waiter could be devastating to him if he has no backup income.

In order to remain outside of bad faith, we have to acknowledge both our own freedom and our facticity, the factors that limit that freedom. We also must acknowledge that in spite of these constraints we are always making a choice. We often avoid taking on the responsibility that comes with being free and find it easier to be told what to do or have a pre-given identity to fall back on. Rather than accept the difficult path of creating one's own project, people tend to hide from their freedom and tell themselves they have no other options. This is how they avoid accountability for the choices they make, including choices that cause harm to others.

Bad faith is all too common, and all of us are guilty of it from time to time. Authors such as David Detmer have pointed out that the same tools we use to deceive others are the tools we use to deceive ourselves. For example, we often use selective attention, partial information, or omission rather than outright lies. WikiLeaks often involves exposing not only unethical or unjust behavior, but the evidence of wrongdoing that was intentionally hidden or destroyed. It's likely for at least some of these individuals that in order to participate they had to convince themselves either that they weren't doing anything wrong or that they had no other choice. However, when their behavior is there for inter-pretation from another—an Other—the tools they were using to deceive themselves are less likely to deceive the Other.

The Bad Faith of Bad Behavior

WikiLeaks is concerned with exposing bad behavior by powerful individuals. Let's examine how bad faith plays a role in taking actions we know are wrong. Suppose I receive an order from an administrator to electronically delete and shred paper documents related to my department's finances for a two-month period (purely hypothetical!). The request immediately seems odd to me, so before fulfilling it I glance through the documents in question. As I'm skimming, I come across charges to the website phonydiploma.com, a site known to sell fake diplomas and transcripts.

It's clear to an outside observer that someone used department money to buy evidence of a fake degree, and at least one administrator is aware of it and trying to cover it up (again, all hypothetical!). I know that the ethical thing to do would be to report the charges to the higher ups so someone is held accountable. Instead, I delete the electronic documents and make my way over to the shredder.

Now, I will certainly try to justify this decision to myself—either by trying to convince myself that I'm not doing anything wrong or that I have no other choice. For example, I might tell myself, "The order to destroy the documents probably has nothing to do with the charges from that website. It's possible that it's completely unrelated." Or, I might say, "It's likely that a student somehow was able to use department funds to buy a fake diploma." Or, "The administration has likely dealt with this internally and ordered me to destroy the documents so that they're not publicly embarrassed. It would be horrible for everyone who works here to have that information made public." Or, even if I admit to myself that I'm obviously destroying evidence of wrongdoing, I might say, "My role as an employee of this university requires this. I have no other choice." I would likely tell myself, "It's the fault of those who bought the diploma and those trying to cover it up, not mine."

All of these statements are examples of Sartrean bad faith—I'm either denying the facticity of the situation, or I'm denying my freedom not to participate. In either case, I refuse to take responsibility for the role I choose to play in hiding evidence. These misleading half-truths allow me to convince myself that the only thing I can possibly do is put the documents in the shredder.

Enter the Other

Now imagine that as I'm getting ready to shred the documents a colleague walks into the room unexpectedly. She asks me what I'm doing, and suddenly the lie I've been telling myself becomes harder to believe. I could try to lie about my motives, but the shredder's already on, and it's clear that I'm about to shred the documents. The paths I saw laid out for me and the stories I told myself are all suddenly subject to interpretation by an Other, another free person. Forced to admit what I'm doing to my co-worker, the lie I've been telling myself is no longer believable. At the deepest level, I knew all along I was choosing to shred documents to cover up some wrongdoing. When I'm forced to admit to her what I was about to do, I'm also forced to admit it to myself. *This* is the power of being observed by an Other—we realize that our actions are subject to the *judgment* of another free person.

If I were to remain outside of bad faith, I would be forced to admit to myself, "I choose to work at this university, and it provides me with my livelihood. I don't want to lose this livelihood. The consequences of refusing to participate in my institution's wrongdoing are too much for me, so I'm going to shred these documents to please the administrator and erase the record of harms caused. I'm *complicit* in the wrongdoing based on my free choice."

From this example, it's clear why bad faith is often the easier path than accepting what we know to be true at a deeper level. But, we also see how being observed by an Other makes it more difficult to carry through with my plan and more difficult to lie to myself about my actions. The Sartrean viewpoint applied to this small-scale situation involving a few actors has the same structure as what takes place when powerful individuals commit wrongdoing and it becomes the interest of WikiLeaks.

A Virtual Other

On WikiLeaks's website, they describe themselves as specializing in "the analysis and publication of large datasets of censored or otherwise restricted official materials involving war, spying, and corruption." WikiLeaks prides themselves on being a news source that accepts anonymous information, verifies it, and releases the information so the public can make their own judgments. Their website now lists six categories of leaks, including "Intelligence," "Global Economy," "International Politics," "Corporations," "Government," and "War and Military."

Before the existence of WikiLeaks, when powerful individuals considered whether or not to participate in behavior they knew was unjust or immoral, they only had to worry about keeping their actions hidden from immediate contacts. They had to make sure those few people who were witness to their behavior were too scared to go public with the information because they had too much to lose by doing so. An existential choice was made within this set of conditions. Of course, there have always been exceptions to this rule, the truly courageous whistleblowers who, in true Sartrean fashion, refused to live in bad faith.

Now, however, the threat of exposure by WikiLeaks has added a new dimension to the choice. People can ultimately be tried not only in a courtroom, but in the court of public opinion. In some cases, the threat of WikiLeaks will influence someone's decision not to participate in a scheme of wrongdoing. Not only would they be acting immorally, but they may be subject to public shaming and humiliation. This added dimension likely contributes to a hesitance to participate in unethical behavior or an increased care in making sure the "trail" of one's wrongdoing is erased from cyberspace. Additionally, it may lead to more scrutiny of who's privy to information and to less willingness to trust others. In any case, if someone wants to build an existential project as one who is engaged in corruption and wrong-doing, WikiLeaks has clearly muddied the waters.

WikiLeaks introduces a Sartrean Other who's watching even when we aren't directly confronted with an Other in our physical environment, a *virtual* Other. In the example of shredding documents, my freedom was interrupted when an Other entered the room and my actions became subject to her interpretation. With the threat of WikiLeaks, powerful individuals are threatened by the gaze of the Other *at all times*. However, this Other isn't just the immediate physical threat of one Other, but the virtual presence of a million Others.

The threat of exposure also may force powerful individuals to admit to aspects of their behavior that they otherwise might deny. If a governor is considering accepting a bribe, he would have to accept that he's acting illegally or immorally when he decides to follow through and accept the bribe. The increased care a person must take when covering their tracks forces them to admit on a deeper level the true motivations behind their actions. Thus, individuals must accept an increased responsibility for what they are going to do. The consideration of how this will look in the public eye forces them to admit new dimensions of their choice. If they do follow through and have their behavior exposed by WikiLeaks, they're forced to accept their own accountability. They're forced to admit to themselves and to others what they previously had been trying to deny. All the same, sometimes they look for new reasons to justify their actions. But these reasons don't only have to convince *them*; they're submitted to the scrutiny of a million Others.

Shenanigans Revealed

In the 2016 Democratic primary between Hillary Clinton and Senator Bernie Sanders, Sanders's supporters called foul, arguing that the Democratic National Committee was intentionally favoring Hillary Clinton. Voters argued that DNC officials intentionally limited the number of debates and stacked over four hundred superdelegate votes for Hillary Clinton before even a single vote had been cast. Throughout the primary, DNC chairwoman Debbie Wasserman-Schultz and other members of the Democratic leadership repeatedly told the public that no favoritism existed and they were running a fair and impartial primary.

However, after the race was over and Hillary Clinton was deemed the winner, WikiLeaks released emails from several powerful individuals working for the DNC that showed evidence of favoritism toward Hillary Clinton: emails revealing the Clinton campaign had been privately given debate questions before the debates, DNC officials conspiring to frame Sanders as an atheist in public to discourage voters, and brainstorming ways to construct negative narratives about Sanders's campaign. The emails revealed that powerful individuals in the DNC were far from impartial and were, as many voters believed, trying to sway the race in favor of Hillary Clinton.

It's likely that officials in the DNC justified this behavior to themselves, either by denying that their actions truly constituted favoritism, denying their actions were having any effect on the outcome, or telling themselves that the possibility that Sanders would lose the general election or that Hillary Clinton would make a better president justified what they were doing. DNC staffers on the lower end of the power structure likely told themselves that their jobs depended on Clinton winning, and thus that they had no choice. It's also likely that the official narrative circulating around the Democratic leadership was that the primary was actually fair, and the means of favoritism were subtle enough that many could argue it didn't indicate a failure to be impartial. A debate question here or there, no big deal, right?

Primary voters filed a lawsuit against the DNC with the charge that they had donated to Senator Sanders's campaign under the false pretense that leadership were remaining neutral. Democrats responded not by denying the accusations (the evidence was there!) but instead by arguing that they were *under no obligation to be fair*: "There is no right to—just by virtue of making a donation, to enforce the parties' internal rules," said DNC attorney

Bruce Spiva. "And there's no right to not have your candidate disadvantaged or have another candidate advantaged." No longer able to lie to the public, they were forced to admit the truth behind their actions and make their reasons open to judgment by the Other.

People certainly disagree as to whether Bernie Sanders or Hillary Clinton should've won, and on whether or not a political party has the moral obligation to run an impartial primary, but what this example shows is that the exposure by WikiLeaks of behind the scenes behavior forced Democratic officials to stop denying the motivations behind their actions. Like the colleague who forced me to admit the truth of my intentions in shredding the documents, the exposure of their private emails to the public forced Democratic officials to admit the favoritism in the primary. With the argument that they were not obligated to host a fair primary, the reasons for their actions are subject to scrutiny by millions of people.

Whether you love them or hate them, WikiLeaks isn't going away any time soon. As WikiLeaks continues to play a role in our modern social and political landscape, more powerful individuals will be pre-emptively looking for ways to cover their tracks and planning what stories to tell the public. While planning for these possibilities, they're less likely to be in bad faith regarding the nature of their actions. Some might choose not to engage in the actions at all. If their wrongdoing is eventually exposed to the public, they'll be held accountable for their free choices by others and themselves.

WikiLeaks has changed the existential conditions through which modern people choose their projects and introduced a powerful new mechanism of accountability, a virtual Other.

Sixth Dump

Know It All

12
On the Disadvantage of WikiLeaks for Life

Leslie A. Aarons

The mission of WikiLeaks, we are told, is to dis-seminate highly classified information from powerful global organizations and individuals to serve the public interest. WikiLeaks's stated goal is:

> to bring important news and information to the public . . . One of our most important activities is to publish original source material . . . so readers and historians alike can see evidence of the truth.

Serving as a populist, dissident intelligence operation, WikiLeaks divulges confidential information about formidable institutions to the public. Julian Assange claims that his organization serves the public's right to know and promotes the First Amendment to the US Constitution by disclosing evidence of corruption and collusion of powerful individuals and organizations. However, the question remains whether readers and historians are actually benefiting from WikiLeaks's mission and methodologies.

In an interview with the *New York Times* published August 31st 2016, Assange stated that WikiLeaks works to verify whatever material it's given in service of the public, which, as he stated, "loves it when they get a glimpse into the corrupt machinery that is attempting to rule them." However, WikiLeaks has been accused of a number of disreputable practices that throw its proclaimed duty and the soundness of its publications into question. These criticisms include probes into the degree to which WikiLeaks strategically times the release of intelligence it has obtained, withholding and disseminating secret files to serve what some claim is Assange's personal political agenda.

WikiLeaks has also been criticized for editing content without transparency, and at other times, for its refusal to redact information that puts innocent third parties in jeopardy. And these substantial controversies are further exacerbated by Assange's own legal turmoil that continues to plague him and threatens the legitimacy of his entire mission.

Trumping all of these significant concerns is Assange's steadfast assumption that by revealing evidence of clandestine hypocrisy and corruption of dominant governmental forces to the public, WikiLeaks serves as a social and political counterforce for justice. But is this actually true? Is the revelation of such information serving the public good?

No doubt WikiLeaks's mission assumes the adage that "information is power," but the question is whether this barrage of damning covert information serves as a catalyst for individual justice or social progress *at all*.

A Danger to Society

The historical audit always brings to light so much that is false, crude, inhuman, absurd, violent, that the attitude of pious illusion, in which alone all that wants to live can live, is necessarily dispelled.

—Friedrich Nietzsche

German philosopher Friedrich Nietzsche (1844–1900) can offer stunning insight into this question. In his essay, "On the Advantage and Disadvantage of History for Life," Nietzsche identifies the dangers that present themselves when a society and its people become too obsessed with the chronicling of human activity as an end in itself: "there is a degree of insomnia, of rumination, of historical sense which injures every living thing and finally destroys it, be it a man, a people or a culture."

Informed by Nietzsche's essay, we can argue that WikiLeaks is in fact a danger to society, in that it over-estimates the value of the information it discloses as well as the public's ability to critically process that information and, by so doing, it undermines the demand and the drive for much needed social progress.

Nietzsche believes that philosophy's greatest power lies in how it inspires the individual to live a passionate and meaningful life. It's true that the discipline of philosophy concerns knowledge, truth, and history; but for Nietzsche, how to *apply* such philosophical knowledge in order to live a self-determining and creative existence is philosophy's highest achievement. Nietzsche decisively evaluates the usefulness of history for inspiring contemporary action. He argues that history—the chronicle of human actions and events—provides essential inspiration that enables us to live a life emboldened by wisdom, courage, and compassion.

One way that history inspires us is how it exemplifies individuals that have been capable of great and courageous achievements. Take for example how Dr. Martin Luther King Jr. persevered through seemingly insurmountable racial hatred and inequality, successfully challenging extreme prejudice and inequitable laws, using his own distinctive strategy of non-violent protest, and by his eloquent speeches inspired by his personal faith. History immortalizes such individuals and prompts us to realize that the incredible fortitude that was once demonstrated by others is potentially attainable by us as well.

But Nietzsche's critique of history is foremost a cautionary tale, and he warns that history can also be extremely dangerous to life when it's misused and misconstrued. Actions and events can be taken out of the pertinent context in which they occurred, and the documentation and interpretation of events could undoubtedly be intentionally or inadvertently dubious. Historical accounts can be distorted and used as propaganda, deceiving audiences and misrepresenting the truth to serve nefarious ends. By utilizing Nietzsche's critique of history, a number of urgent concerns about WikiLeaks present themselves. One of these is whether WikiLeaks conveys the truth, the whole truth and nothing but the truth.

His Colleagues Have Turned Against Him

The problem is that WikiLeaks—whose mission statement was "to produce . . . a more just society . . . based upon truth"—has been guilty of the same obfuscation and misinformation as those it sought to expose, while its supporters are expected to follow, unquestioningly, in blinkered, cultish devotion.

—JEMIMA KHAN

WikiLeaks is an offspring of the Internet; a newfangled source of news that chronicles assorted secret activities of powerful entities. It came into full prominence in 2010 when it released more than 250,000 top-secret US State Department cables. Its web-based platform utilizes the reach of the World Wide Web to both receive covert information donated by unidentified sources and to release this intelligence to the public. Its mission declares that the revelation of this concealed information to the public is a springboard for social progress.

When the associate editor of the *New Statesman* wrote the article, "Jemima Khan on Julian Assange: How the Wikileaks Founder Alienated His Allies," her research found that many of Julian Assange's colleagues have turned against him, criticizing his motives and practices. Many pundits, even from rival political camps, are in agreement that Assange—who persistently claims, "I am WikiLeaks"—seems to be led more by his ego, a skewed political bent, and personal vendettas than by transparency and a clear sense of justice.

Julian Assange has made it crystal clear that he despises Hillary Clinton, for example. He has maligned her as a corrupt, self-serving war-monger: "Hillary's problem is not just that she's a war hawk. She's a war hawk with bad judgment who gets an unseemly emotional rush out of killing people. She shouldn't be let near a gun shop, let alone an army. And she certainly should not become president of the United States."

Assange claims he formulated his opinion regarding Hillary Clinton based on his study of thousands of her incriminating State Department emails. But Assange's critique of Clinton goes well beyond politically-minded contempt—it's *personal*. Assange has made claims that he believes Hillary Clinton has directly wielded her power to harm WikiLeaks and himself personally. "Hillary Clinton is receiving constant updates about my personal situation; she has pushed for the prosecution of WikiLeaks," he told ITV. "We do see her as more of a problem for freedom of the press generally." Assange views Clinton as an undemocratic imperialist who directly threatens the welfare of his organization and his own personal well-being.

As the saying goes, "timing is everything." And there is direct evidence that Assange used his access to covert information to plan a tactical strike against Hillary Clinton, intended to severely harm her. *Six weeks before*

WikiLeaks published an archive of hacked Democratic National Committee (DNC) emails, and released them on the eve of the Democratic National Convention, Assange admitted that he was already in possession of thousands of classified emails that Clinton sent illegally over her private server, and that they were highly incriminating.

He had yet to release the emails, and it appeared that he was instead strategically calculating their release to do the greatest harm to Hillary Clinton's chances of winning the presidency. Assange told British television host Robert Peston of the ITV network that WikiLeaks had obtained "emails related to Hillary Clinton which are pending publication," which he described as great evidence of her corruption. Assange declared that he not only staunchly opposed her candidacy for President of the United States on policy grounds, but that he also saw her as a personal adversary. At one point, the interviewer, Mr. Peston says: "Plainly, what you are saying, what you are publishing, hurts Hillary Clinton."

Analysts agree that, all told, WikiLeaks's release of the hacked DNC emails and the disclosure of Clinton's misuse of highly classified government information during her tenure as the United States Secretary of State dealt a deadly blow to Clinton's candidacy for President. But, wait, what happened to WikiLeaks's pledge of transparency? WikiLeaks's proletarian secret-busting mission is supposed to fight the hypocrisy of power-mongering parties by leaking covert information that these parties use to wield their power.

WikiLeaks's own transparency is imperative to fight the good fight. But, it's evident from his own admission that in the case of Hillary Clinton and the DNC, Assange was *not* transparent in the timely release of information, and further, used the furtive information he had in his possession to wield his own control and advantage, compounding the duplicity and breaching the public's right to know. This necessarily leads one to wonder how many other instances of WikiLeaks's own corruption abound that threaten the integrity of its status and its mission.

History in Context

Monumental history deceives with analogies: with tempting similarities the courageous are enticed to rashness, the enthusiastic to fanaticism; and if one thinks of this history as being in the hands and heads of talented egoists and enraptured rascals then empires are destroyed, princes murdered, wars and revolutions instigated.

—FRIEDRICH NIETZSCHE

Merely being informed about historic news and information, without the ability to appreciate the complex nuances and intricate dynamics that are always involved in the occurrence of these events, is ultimately counterproductive and dangerous to social and political progress. Being cognizant about random cryptic minutiae of iconic individuals and events as an end in itself adds little to the social or political advancement of human society, and quite possibly may cause unanticipated collateral damage.

Nietzsche criticized such obsessive, idle historiographers, referring to them as "superhistorical" malingerers. He writes that:

the superhistorical thinker illuminates all history of peoples and individuals from within, clairvoyantly guesses the original significance of the different hieroglyphs and gradually evades, as one fatigued, the incessant flow of new script: how could he fail, amid the endless superfluity of events, to take in his fill, and finally be nauseated!

By Nietzsche's estimation, a society will become sickened by its obsession with history. This cultural fixation on historical accounting undermined what he called the vital "plastic power" of man: "I mean the power distinctively to grow out of itself, transforming and assimilating everything past and alien, to heal wounds, replace what is lost, and reshape broken forms out of itself." Nietzsche argues that the overly zealous fixation on historical accounting has an atrophying effect, in that contemporary events, which are not yet historically memorialized, seem petty and unimportant because they lack the prominence and the retrospective wisdom bestowed by history.

But all people and events memorialized by history were inspired by incredibly multifaceted contexts, the chronicling of which is rarely appreciated or even understood. What was going on in the mind of General George Washington when he accepted the charge of Congress in 1775 to take command of the Continental Army to overwhelm the British in Boston? General Washington had little practice handling large, conventional armies, yet he proved to be a skillful leader of the American military forces during the war. Although he lost more battles than he won, Washington employed cunning strategies that included a number of monumental victories. But one of Washington's most venerated decisions was to surrender his commission to Congress, affirming the principle of civilian control of the military in the newly formed United States that poignantly changed the course of US history.

How can we fathom the fortitude and misgivings of this one man? History cannot comport his personal resilience or his cognitions. History can merely offer general portraits of men that fail to capture the contexts—the mania and doubts that fuel the making of such history. What is the cost-benefit analysis of leaking an isolated moment of a long, contemptuous military battle; a transcript of a phone conversation; evidence of an inappropriate use of a communication device; names and events amputated from their contexts? These can easily be misconstrued a thousand ways by purveyors of such history.

Assange the Freedom Fighter

All who spend time in the spy world soon come to the view that the rest of the population lives their life in a sea fog as a tiny piece of cork buffeted by a vast ocean of concealed truth.

—JULIAN ASSANGE

Assange proclaims himself to be a devoted messenger in service to the masses. He regards the public as being uninformed victims, ignorant of the malevolent empires that maliciously wield their power to control and exploit them for their own enrichment.

In a blog post entitled, "The Non-linear Effects of Leaks on Unjust Systems of Governance," Assange argues: "Only revealed injustice can be answered; for man to do anything intelligent he has to know what's actually going on." WikiLeaks is a platform for Assange's mission of cyber-espionage, whose goal is to gain illicit access to confidential information held by powerful government entities. He promotes himself as a kind of modern day Robin Hood or Freedom Fighter, stealing from the rich and the corrupt to give to the huddled masses yearning to breathe free.

WikiLeaks serves as a reservoir for secrets obtained by hackers who target secure computer networks, breaking clandestine codes and gaining access to classified information. Hackers are modern day pirates voyaging cyberspace, breaking and entering, spying and stealing to obtain their bounty. Their treasures are gleaned by penetrating the security that was set in place to protect these private systems. As a result of this theft of private property, owners are often left vanquished and vulnerable.

Assange aids and abets this illegal activity by providing a repository where hackers may anonymously deposit their ill-gotten information. Assange himself claims not to be a party to these cybercrimes when they are committed, but he may indeed have prior knowledge of specific targets of such espionage, and he certainly has complicity in their occurrence, by encouraging them and by creating a market for their value.

Mission Compromised

> And now a quick glance at our time! We are shocked, we fly back: whither is all clarity, all naturalness and purity of that relation between life and history, how confused, how exaggerated, how troubled is this problem which now surges before our eyes!
>
> —FRIEDRICH NIETZSCHE

Is it possible to justify this illegal enterprise that emboldens unethical activity, as a necessary evil in the fight for Justice? Assange claims it is. He claims that WikiLeaks offers evidence of the truth. Employing the maxim "the truth shall set you free," the premise of Assange's argument and his prima facie defense of WikiLeaks rests on the reliability and the validity of the information it releases to the public. The veracity of WikiLeaks's releases is of the utmost importance in determining and establishing its utility and justifying the soundness of its mission. So how reliable are the contents of its releases?

In a TEDtalk interview with Julian Assange in 2010, titled, "Why the World Needs WikiLeaks," Assange was asked about his knowledge of the informants who donate the pilfered, top-secret information that WikiLeaks disseminates to the public. He stated, "... so these are—as far as we can tell—they are classical whistle-blowers." This response is woefully inadequate, and extremely disconcerting. If WikiLeaks is unable to identify and confirm the sources of the information that it receives, then their entire mission is irredeemably compromised.

But this is in fact the case. Assange continues to explain in the interview that WikiLeaks purposefully employs state of the art encryption to protect the identities of these "classical whistle-blowers" who feed WikiLeaks its intelligence. The interview continues:

> **INTERVIEWER:** So you make an effort to ensure the documents are legitimate, but you actually almost never know who the identity of the source is?
>
> **ASSANGE:** That's right, yeah. Very rarely do we ever know, and if we find out at some stage then we destroy that information as soon as possible.

So, how does WikiLeaks determine that the sources of information are not illegitimate zealots, or hate-mongering extremist organizations, or fraudulent opportunists with malevolent agendas, who are taking advantage of WikiLeaks, to plant fake news to serve their own disreputable schemes? Assange's response offers little insight into this all-important question.

Creative Direction

> But history which only destroys without being guided by an inner constructive drive will in the long run make its instruments blasé and unnatural: for such men destroy illusions and whoever destroys illusion in himself and others will be punished by nature, the strictest tyrant.
>
> —FRIEDRICH NIETZSCHE

Apparently, Assange is either unwilling or unable to verify the credibility of the sources of the information that he himself endorses by releasing it to the public. This is at the very least a cause for great concern and at the very worst possibly indicative of his own self-serving corruption. WikiLeaks claims to be forcing transparency out of powerful and controlling agencies that covertly dupe and exploit the public. Specifically, WikiLeaks argues that the public has the right to know of the inherent corruption and abuse that's always at work in these agencies and how they ultimately wield their power to victimize citizens and render the public impotent and at their mercy.

As a remedy for such tyranny, WikiLeaks allows the public to gain access by streaming a record of assorted, allegedly unethical and illegal events, whose scope and veracity remains questionable. But, how exactly is such information promoting justice for individuals?

Is there bound to be corruption in societies? Yes. Are there covert operations at work in the world that intentionally deny public access? No doubt. Is having such corruption corroborated and displayed by WikiLeaks beneficial to the public's interest? Not necessarily.

A case in point is WikiLeaks's release of a classified US military video depicting the killing of people in the Iraqi suburb of New Baghdad. WikiLeaks produced a polished, movie-like, narrated production around the military video footage that was shot from the leading Apache helicopter gun-sight. WikiLeaks released an edited, shorter version (17:46) as well as the "full unedited gun-camera video" footage (39:13). The dramatic title that WikiLeaks gave these productions is "Collateral Murder."

The footage is indeed disturbing. The ravages of war always are. Adding to the unnerving visual footage that WikiLeaks poignantly subtitled is the audio recording of the military communications. We hear the military helicopter pilots deducing what they believe to be men with weapons in the war-torn Iraqi city. According to WikiLeaks, the men in the pilot's sights are actually professional photographers chronicling the war. The video explains in the subtitled narration and audio transcript, that the pilots are misidentifying the cameras that the men are holding, as being weapons:

01:21   That's a weapon.
01:22   Yeah.
01:23   Hotel Two-Six; Crazy Horse One-Eight [*second Apache helicopter*].
01:32   Fucking prick.
01:33   Hotel Two-Six this is Crazy Horse One-Eight [*communication between chopper 1 and chopper 2*]. Have individuals with weapons.
01:41   Yup. He's got a weapon too.
01:43   Hotel Two-Six; Crazy Horse One-Eight. Have five to six individuals with AK47s [*automatic rifles*]. Request permission to engage [*shoot*].
01:51   Roger that. Uh, we have no personnel east of our position. So, uh, you are free to engage. Over.
02:00   All right, we'll be engaging.
02:02   Roger, go ahead.
02:10   He's got an RPG [*Rocket Propelled Grenade*].
02:11   All right, we got a guy with an RPG.
02:13   I'm gonna fire.
02:14   Okay.

The average civilian will cringe and writhe when watching this production. Like in a horror movie when the protagonist doesn't see the monster around that next corner, the spectator wants to shout, "Look out!" to no avail. The footage shows all the gory details, men dropping to the ground, the shocking sound and fury of gunfire, individual's stationary bodies lying in the mass of debris. There's even footage of one of the shooting victims mortally wounded but trying in vain to crawl for cover. The pilots are heard admiring their work:

04:31   Oh, yeah, look at those dead bastards.
04:36   Nice.
04:37   Two-Six; Crazyhorse One-Eight.
04:44   Nice.
04:47   Good shoot.
04:48   Thank you.

This WikiLeaks production does far more than report the facts characteristic of investigative journalism. It imposes on the audience a specific plot and summary designed to influence the public's experience. "Collateral Murder" opens to a black frame with a quote from none other than George Orwell. In bright white words it reads: "Political language is designed to make lies sound truthful, and to give the appearance of solidity to pure wind." The production is complete with rolling credits at the end. The first credit is to "Our courageous source," and the second credit names Julian Assange, as the producer and creative director. Does such an episode need creative direction? Is the public so naive that it cannot comprehend this event, without it being high-lighted and sculpted by Julian Assange? It appears here that history is providing a grand stage for self-promotion.

Nietzsche's insightful critique of the advantages and disadvantages of history shows it to be a tightrope walk, where careful balance is imperative and peril is always a misstep away. From this precipice we may wonder whether the history that WikiLeaks presents inspires and promotes a higher social conscience.

Or, does it rather contribute to the disenfranchisement and disillusionment of people already overwhelmed and revolted by too much information?

13
Is There Too Much Information?

Louis Colombo

If knowledge is power, then we might think that more knowledge, or more information, would equal more power. We might then think, as consumers of information, that we would always be better off with more information, and never with less.

So, the question, "Is there too much information?", may sound a bit ridiculous, just as if someone asked whether we can have too much money. In both cases, and especially since money is yet another road to power, the only possible answer to the question "How much money or information do you want?" would be "More." And not just "more," but "always more."

Is More Always Better?

Is this intuitive answer the correct one? While we won't concern ourselves with the question of whether or not there is too much money (certainly not in this author's bank account), we will ask the question about information.

For looking around at our current media landscape, saturated as it is with the twenty-four hour news cycle that demands to be filled, not just on TV (network and cable), but radio as well, running commentaries on social media sites like Facebook and Twitter, newspapers and news magazines (both print and digital), blogs, vlogs, and now WikiLeaks, we might begin to wonder whether we are truly better off with the flood of information now at our disposal.

In the laundry list of media outlets that I've mentioned, and perhaps even those that I've left out, WikiLeaks is unique in that it functions not as a "traditional" news source that simply reports on the day's events with varying levels of interpretative slant, but as an online platform dedicated to publishing leaked and otherwise classified information. On its website, WikiLeaks boldly lays out in its mission statement that it "specializes in the analysis and publication of large datasets of censored or otherwise restricted official materials involving war, spying, and corruption." A visit to the WikiLeaks home page gives users the opportunity to explore leaked documents grouped under several headings: Intelligence, Global Economy, International Politics, Corporations, Government, and War and Military.

As an example of the kind of material WikiLeaks publishes, on August 24th 2017 WikiLeaks published "Vault 7," a series of secret documents of the cyber-operations of the CIA against its liaison intelligence services, including the NSA, the DHS, and the FBI. Other documents include secret tapes and transcripts, policy documents, trade deals, email exchanges, transcribed meeting records, and the like. By way of understanding the scale and ambitions of WikiLeaks's publishing record, in the eleven years of its existence, WikiLeaks has published roughly one million censored or restricted datasets per year.

This is a staggering amount of information, none of which was intended for public consumption, now made available and easily searchable for anyone with access to a computer. Without dealing with the whole of the media spectacle, we can now ask with respect to WikiLeaks in particular, "Is there too much information? Has WikiLeaks published too much?"

The Greatest Good for the Greatest Number

One approach to answering these questions may be found in utilitarian ethics. Although ethical insights that would later be associated with utilitarianism can already be found in thinkers such as Epicurus (341–270 B.C.E.), the earliest formal presentation of what we now call utilitarianism can be found in Jeremy Bentham's *An Introduction to the Principles of Morals and Legislation,* published in 1789.

Utilitarianism begins with the observation that people generally seek their own good. In other words, people generally act in ways that they believe will bring them pleasure, while simultaneously avoiding pain. Of course, someone might appear to act contrary to this. For example, many people find strenuous exercise painful, and yet gym memberships, particularly after New Year's, suggest that many people willingly undergo such displeasure. In response, utilitarian thinkers would point out that people who find exercise painful but who do it anyway, do so not for the pain, but for the health or aesthetic benefits that they believe will follow.

This means that we don't pursue pain for its own sake, but only for the pleasure that results from the pain. It's delayed gratification. We put up with the pain because we believe it will be outweighed by the pleasure. If we're successful in achieving and maintaining this pleasure over pain, then we have attained happiness, as happiness here is understood, contrary to some other conceptions of happiness (for example, a life of virtue, or blessed union with the divine), as simply the state in which overall pleasure outweighs overall pain.

So far, we have presented a merely *descriptive* view of the way utilitarian thinkers believe that people do *in fact* act, and not yet a *prescriptive* view of the way people *ought* to act, which is to say a normative ethical theory. To be a normative ethical theory, it should tell us not simply how people *do act*, but how they *should act*. An ethical theory is not descriptive, but prescriptive. This is where utilitarianism proves innovative. If it's true that people are motivated to seek their own good, and that good is a balance of pleasure over pain, then, according to the utilitarians, what we *should do* is to promote the greatest good for the greatest number of people.

Can the Ends Really Justify the Means?

While several critics have pointed out the difficulty in moving from a description of what is the case to a prescription of what ought to be the case, the ethical thrust of utilitarian thinking is consequentialist, which means that it measures the rightness of an action not by the intention that motivated it but by the effects it produces. When measuring the rightness of an act, we should determine whether that act produced the greatest amount of happiness for the greatest number of people affected by that act, as compared with other possible actions we could have taken. In this sense, utilitarianism (as well as all forms of consequentialism) is backward-looking.

In practical terms, if I'm contemplating one of several courses of action, the utilitarian approach tells me to look at the consequences that *would* result from each choice I might make and evaluate which action would produce the most pleasure for the most people while simultaneously causing the least amount of pain. For utilitarianism, the individual making the decision of which course of action to follow can't, morally speaking, count their own happiness as any more valuable than the happiness of any other indivdual affected by the action. It might turn out that the morally correct thing to do is to sacrifice my own happiness for the greater good of all those affected by my choice.

Although we should steer clear of many of the weeds of interpretation, there are two particular weeds that we should wade into. The first is a distinction between *act* and *rule* approaches to utilitarianism. An attentive reader will have noticed my emphasis on measuring the "rightness of an act." According to this approach, I must take each particular act as its own unique case as I conduct my "cost-benefit" analysis. This is called act utilitarianism. For example, suppose Maxine and Charles are put into situations where it appears that telling a lie would be expedient. According to act utilitarianism, although both Maxine and Charles are both considering telling a lie, each must evaluate the consequences of their decision individually. Maxine's lie isn't Charlie's lie, and neither has any bearing on the other. These are separate events entailing their own unique set of consequences. It's perfectly possible that Maxine's lie would be right, because it resulted in a surplus of pleasure over pain, whereas Charlie's lie would be wrong because it causes more pain than pleasure. Neither Maxine nor Charlie is morally permitted to weigh their own happiness as more valuable than anyone else's.

By contrast, rule utilitarianism, noticing that both Maxine and Charlie are contemplating the same action, telling a lie, would suggest that we apply the utilitarian calculus not to particular acts, but to species of acts that are governed by a rule. Instead of asking whether Maxine or Charlie ought to lie in their own particular situations, rule utilitarians ask whether lying, if adopted as a general policy, would promote the greatest good for the greatest number. What if everyone lied? Would such a state of affairs produce more or less happiness than one in which no one lied?

If it turns out that lying would promote a surplus of pain over pleasure, then rule utilitarianism would conclude that lying is wrong. It would be wrong because the general principle itself promotes more unhappiness than happiness. But, what about exceptions to the rule? Isn't it sometimes justifiable to break the rule? If so, then rule utilitarianism would collapse into act utilitarianism, albeit our calculus would typically be more efficient, since exceptions to the rule are relatively rare.

The second interpretative weed that we should call attention to concerns the weighing of various types of pleasure. One debate within utilitarian circles concerns the conflict between the quantity and the quality of pleasure. For example, simple amusements may make many people happy, although those amusements may prove to be passively enjoyed and relatively short lived. A rigorous education may reach fewer people, but for those who have both the access to and aptitude for it, such an education could provide a wealth of actively pursued, long lived pleasure. If we had to choose between providing either simple amusements or a rigorous education, and we could only choose one, which should it be? Are the pleasures gained from a rigorous education qualitatively superior to those gained from passive amusement? If so, what makes them better? Better to and for whom?

John Stuart Mill (1806–1873), an eloquent defender of utilitarianism, argued that we could make qualitative distinctions between types of pleasures, that for one who had the opportunity to experience competing pleasures, an appreciation of the inherent qualities of each would guide the "experienced judge" towards those that were qualitatively superior, famously declaring that "it would be better to be a Socrates dissatisfied than a pig satisfied." For the sake of our presentation, we will side with Mill, agreeing that pleasures vary not only in quantity but also in quality. Properly formulated, utilitarianism would have us promote the greatest amount of high quality pleasures, while simultaneously limiting pain, for the greatest number of people.

Utili-Leaking?

Applying this theory to WikiLeaks, we might come up with a simple way to determine whether or not any particular cache of documents ought to be published. We could ask on a case by case basis, like act utilitarianism, whether publishing any particular cache of documents would promote more happiness for more people than not publishing it. But here we immediately run into a difficult problem with utilitarian thinking. How wide do we cast our net when conducting our analysis? Ostensibly, the greatest number of people affected. But, how far into the future must we look, tracing the consequences of any one particular act? Even if we could overcome these hurdles, how are we to determine who has been made happy, who unhappy, and with what relative degree of "high quality pleasures?"

During the run-up to the 2016 United States presidential election, WikiLeaks published a cache of emails connected to the Clinton campaign. While some blame WikiLeaks for Hillary Clinton's loss to Donald Trump, establishing cause in this case is no easy feat. Furthermore, even if it could be determined that publishing the emails cost Clinton the election, the divided US electorate makes it almost impossible to determine whether this contributed to the "greatest good for the greatest number."

Given this difficulty in act utilitarianism, we might ask whether a rules-based approach would be more helpful. One immediate difficulty in applying a rules-based approach is determining what the rule in question is. Should we ask whether publishing information, as a general rule, would make more people happy than unhappy? But this seems too wide. Given that WikiLeaks specializes in publishing classified and secret documents, we might limit our rule to one concerning only those types of documents and ask, "As a rule, does publishing secret and classified documents make more people happy than unhappy?" While friends of transparency might instinctively say "yes," individuals involved in government, business, and any area of life that involves sensitive negotiations might be hesitant to agree.

Even proponents of transparency might balk at the thought of making every classified and secret document public. In a political context, is it likely to contribute to the "greatest good for the greatest number" to make our secret communications available to hostile foreign powers? So again, it looks like rule utilitarianism cannot help us, and, despite the early promise of utilitarian thinking, we are back where we began, asking, "Is there too much information? Has WikiLeaks published too much?"

Context Is Everything

As we have seen above, one problem with the utilitarian approach is that it attempts to formulate an answer to the question of "too much (or too little)" abstractly, devoid of context. But as the philosopher Aristotle pointed out, "too much and too little" are always relative to the individual and to the situation. Two thousand calories a day may be "just right" for most people, but for an Olympic swimmer training for an important competition, it's "too little," just as for someone attempting to lose weight, that same number of calories might prove to be "too much." If we want to get an answer to our question, we should begin by setting it in context. "Too much information for whom? For what purpose?"

Although unorthodox, WikiLeaks can best be understood as a source of news. Indeed, through various partnerships with more traditional news outlets, WikiLeaks hopes to enable its published documents to be seen by as many people as possible. On a charitable reading, WikiLeaks pursues its publishing agenda not to fulfill any personal vendettas its founder, Julian Assange, might have, but to inform citizens of nation-states around the globe of the opaque dealings of the governments and businesses that impact their lives in profound ways. By publishing secret and confidential documents in their full form, WikiLeaks can be seen as providing valuable information free of the filter that more traditional and corporate owned media or government spokespeople use in their reporting. Given this, we might rephrase the question slightly better: In our current media environment, is WikiLeaks providing too much information? This is better, but it's still missing a crucial component. Too much information *for whom?*

One answer to this question comes immediately to mind, for insofar as WikiLeaks publishes documents that are censored or restricted by government agencies or business concerns, the owners of the original documents would most likely respond, "Yes, WikiLeaks is publishing too much information." It's been restricted precisely to prevent it from being widely distributed. But, this is clearly not WikiLeaks's intended audience. So, we could further refine our question and ask, "Given our media environment, is it too much information for the citizens who are governed by powers that wish them not have access to this material?"

Here then is our question, and in part, the beginning of our answer. But, just as we could not answer the question of "too many calories" apart from the goals of the individual consuming them, so we cannot answer the question of "too much information" without considering the role this information should play in the lives of the citizens "consuming" it.

Do We Do It Dewey's Way?

What then is a citizen? What does it mean to be a citizen? At its bare minimum, to be a citizen is to be a subject with legally recognized rights and responsibilities as a member of a political community. As a multinational media organization, WikiLeaks's primary audiences are the citizens of largely democratic nation-states, whether they be in the Americas, Africa, Eurasia, or the Asian Pacific, that is, citizens who, in ideal circumstances, are not ruled *by* a government or governing body, but who actively engage in the practice of self-governance. Echoing Aristotle, philosopher John Dewey (1859–1952) put it in *The Public and its Problems* that democracy represents "the idea of community life itself."

To be a citizen in a democracy is to be a member of a "great community," a community that finds its life and being in the activity of its members. True self-governance requires more than a popular turn out at the polls on election day. It requires an informed citizenry who possess the knowledge to partake in the management of public and political affairs. It includes an informed vote, but also requires an educated population able to engage on questions of ends, not simply means, a population that possesses the knowledge required not only to consider their own immediate self-interest, but long-range, less personal interests as well. It requires an educated population able to participate in spirited and substantive policy debates, debates that proceed through the give and take of reasons (in a word, through philosophy), not soundbites and "gotcha" questions.

To be a citizen, a member of the "great community" in this sense, is to be held responsible for your actions and choices before other members of the community, to challenge and be challenged, so that through this give and take, we cajole, sometimes gently, other times less so, each member to relinquish unfounded opinion, substituting rational argumentation in its place (again, philosophy). As a virtue, democracy requires that we make ourselves worthy and able to fulfill our role as active participants in the life of the community, and this as a way of life, not merely on election day.

Seen in this light, we might propose an answer to the question of "too much information" by asking whether the information published by WikiLeaks enables us as citizens to better participate in the practice of self-governance. WikiLeaks has made an extraordinary amount of information public that otherwise would have never seen the light of day. If the role of a citizen in a democracy is to actively participate in the self-governance of that democracy, and if two ways that a citizen might exercise that duty are by making informed decisions at the voting booth and holding accountable those elected to serve, then there's a strong case that having more information at one's disposal, especially information that those elected to serve might wish to hide, would better enable one in both those functions.

For example, many of the abuses of the Bush era came to light thanks to the work of WikiLeaks. For anyone sincerely interested in making informed decisions and holding leaders to account, knowledge of these abuses would certainly be welcome. One might also hope that the threat of WikiLeaks might compel better behavior from governments that know they risk having their dirty laundry aired before the court of public opinion. In this sense, we might think of WikiLeaks as serving two roles, informing the public and being a community member with a particularly loud voice calling governments to account.

Too Much Information?

If the restricted nature of much governmental and business policy presents the danger of "too little information" to be corrected by entities such as WikiLeaks, the sheer volume of available information presents its own problems. For information to be useful to the citizen, it can't remain "raw information." Before we can reasonably and responsibly act on any information, that information must be processed and assimilated, contextualized and understood.

Part of the problem here is simply keeping up with the amount of information that's out there. Reading through all of the material published by WikiLeaks alone would take more time than most working people have at their disposal. This says nothing of the time it would take to sift through the material, analyzing it, thinking about, putting it in context of knowledge that we already possess, using it to challenge our received opinions, testing our new ideas, and so forth.

And this is just the information provided by WikiLeaks, to say nothing of all the other sources of information we now have at our disposal. Equal to the difficulties posed by the question of time, there are the difficulties posed by the technical nature of much of this information. Comprehending much of this information would require a sophisticated technical or professional background that most readers are unlikely to possess.

We here come upon two challenges that aren't unique to WikiLeaks, but are brought into sharp focus through our investigation into the question we posed with respect to it:

time and education. We won't solve these problems here, but only suggest that to fulfill the promise of democracy, to return to the average citizen the right and responsibility for self-governance, these two challenges must be met. To be a citizen in the full sense of the word requires that all citizens have sufficient time to take part in this project. This has implications that go beyond the scope of this chapter, but a harried working class without sufficient leisure time to invest in the life of its community will do no better than to cast a minimally informed vote when asked to do so.

Without an education focused on the needs of citizens, and not the wishes of industry, freely available to all, the ability to make sense of the flood of information will be a luxury available to the few, as will full participation in the project of self-governance. Those lacking the time and resources for full and active participation will grow continually alienated from whatever governing body is said to represent them, and they will see themselves as ruled, not as self-governing. Under such conditions, we have a democracy in name only and one that won't exist even in name for very long.

We now come to the answer to our original question. Is there too much information? Yes. But not because the amount of information out there is too great, for *paradoxically*, there is still too little information. Ignoring the media consolidation that presents a semblance of variety, there is still too little information when the important work of government is conducted behind closed doors and inaccessible to the public until after the fact, whether that be the current wrangling in the US over a future health care bill, a wrangling so contentious that US congressmen avoided meeting with their constituents so as not to have to answer any questions, or the now scuppered Trans-Pacific Partnership, a massive trade deal negotiated out of the purview of the American public whose interests it was said to serve.

So, while there's certainly too little information, there is, as we have maintained, equally too much information. Too much, for we have failed to meet the challenges posed to us through an ever-evolving information revolution of which WikiLeaks is surely a part, recognizing in the "information economy" challenges and opportunities in the realm of business, without recognizing the same in the political sphere. But, if the sheer volume of information poses particular challenges to citizens of democratic nations, we find the solution to such challenges in a thought that Dewey held dear. For as Dewey believed, the cure for the ills of democracy is simply "more democracy."

While we might recoil from the irony of meeting "too much information" with "more democracy," surely Dewey's insight holds true. For it's not simply adding more democracy to that which exists, but doubling down on our commitment to democracy as a *way of life*, rethinking how we can expand the promise of real self-governance to all those who live under purported democracies, even as we renew these democracies as models of the "great community" we're still seeking.

Seventh Dump

Street Cred

14
The Conscience of Reality Winner

JENNIFER BAKER

Though we have let her languish in jail, refusing her bond, arguing that her attorneys can't even cite "classified" material that has been published in newspapers, Henry David Thoreau would regard Reality Winner differently. He would thoroughly approve of her (including that name!) and thoroughly disapprove of us. So, what are we doing wrong, and what is Winner doing right?

What would Thoreau say about her acts of civil disobedience, and what broader lessons can we learn about the ethical character of leaking documents by looking at Winner's story? Is there a more thorough accounting of the ethics of leaking? Can leaking be a virtue?

Many of us are familiar with Thoreau from our classes in high school. Maybe he seems a bit antique today, his ideas toothless, his anti-slavery efforts remote. But we can revisit the moral ferocity for which he advocated, in the hopes of getting us to reconsider what we owe Reality Winner, a military veteran and US federal contract employee, who sent the press classified information about Russian attempts to hack American voting machines. Her social media correspondence has itself been released, in which she had expressed outrage at the current administration's "lying." In both of these actions, she met Thoreau's criteria for a moral hero: one who has the courage to follow her conscience.

Is Winner a Moral Loser?

Why, then, is Winner getting nothing like a hero's reception? Right off the bat, we can consider three reasons for thinking Winner deserves her time in jail, unlike Thoreau, who was released after a night, his bond for refusing to pay the poll tax itself paid by admirers of his ethical stance.

First, we might think that Winner is bound by her employment contract in a way that supersedes any call she might have felt to make documents about Russian interference public. Second, we might think that Winner was politically motivated and only interested in sinking the Trump ship of state, and so not doing this for the right reasons. Third, we might think that any approval of Winner could set an example that would destroy the very idea of classified information in government, thereby hurting us all.

Regarding the first reason, business ethicists have been prolific. There's a lot of work that debates the definition of whistleblowing. It often cites some of the empirical work on whistleblowers. They tend to be older, respected, and to work in organizations they have seen address problems before. Winner—young, a veteran (so perhaps respected)— might have had confidence that the US would react to the information she had provided about Russian interference. (Depending on how the Mueller investigation turns out, she may have been right about that.)

What she failed to do is to go through all the proper channels before going public. But what does any of this tell us anyway? Whether her whistleblowing was legitimate or not doesn't seem to be what has made the difference in how the public has failed to support her. (How many in the public keep up with business ethics literature?) What we really want to know is whether Winner was *morally right* to do what she did, and whether the public is *morally wrong* in failing to support her.

The second reason we might not support Reality Winner is that her motives might be political or personal, and therefore impure. Political philosopher Vaclav Havel thought this was a common way to dismiss activists, writing that "the representatives of power invariably come to terms with those who live within the truth by persistently ascribing utilitarian motivations to them—a lust for power or fame or wealth—and thus they try, at least, to implicate them in their own world, the world of general demoralization." And it's a strange way to think about moral motivation. It's certainly not in line with the tradition with which the founders of the United States aligned themselves, one where personal ethics was the proper touchstone for any political proposal.

Winner, finding the political to be moral, is in line with the lofty sentiments of a Tom Paine or an Alexis de Tocqueville. Paine, in *Common Sense*, warned us that if our governments were not kept moral then we're deceiving ourselves and will surely bring "ruin upon posterity." Tocqueville predicted that citizens would lose their desire for freedom over time, letting it be taken from their hands "without resistance, for fear of compromising by any effort the very well-being that they owe to it." He ponders: "What do they lack to make them free? What? The very desire to be so. Do not ask me to analyze this sublime desire, it must be felt." So, we shouldn't dismiss Winner simply because there happens to be a trend of thinking politics is a "neutral" business that it's important to keep separate from personal morality. This trend might be wrong. Thoreau would certainly think so.

The third reason for thinking Winner deserves punishment is that either she is setting a disastrous example that others will follow, or her efforts are inconsistent with the good our government does. These could be made into extended ethical arguments, and surely we could wait until the full consequences of her disclosures have come about: will the government act on the information, or will there be a rash of similar actions taken by contractors with access to classified information? But in the meantime, before any such potentially negatives consequences materialize, let's dwell on the positive side of her behavior. If this side outweighs even *potential* downsides to what Winner has done, we may have made our case.

Zero to Hero

After lecturing on Thoreau's *Civil Disobedience* in an American Philosophy class, I asked some students who had been vocal about opposing Trump why they didn't refuse to pay taxes that year. It is, after all, what Thoreau would have wondered. They gazed at me in the way that indicated my question was being taken seriously, and one finally replied. "Well, that would be effective, I guess . . . at least if it were co-ordinated." Several then began to respond at once, nodding at each other as they agreed that refusing to pay taxes would be "pretty extreme." They seemed to agree that taking that option would be *needlessly* extreme.

But why? Is it that the wrongness of slavery trumps anti-Trumpism? Or would the class have been the moderates that Thoreau so roundly disdained? Such moderates, like Thoreau's neighbors, who verbally agreed that slavery was a great evil but would do nothing costly to end it, have "resigned their conscience to the legislation." For Thoreau, we should never "in the least degree" do this. Rather, we should be "men first, and subjects afterward," because it's not desirable to "cultivate a respect for the law, so much as for the right." He argues that a failure to act against a government that you believe is unethical signals a singular and unforgivable cowardice.

From the looks of it, then, a Thoreauvian case is made for Winner's heroism. His support is obvious. He wouldn't need any more evidence than that she risked herself in order to heed her conscience. Her employment contract would not matter to him, her being politically-motivated would seem right to him, and the idea that her acting on conscience could constitute or bring some type of harm to our polity is at odds with what he maintained to be true about conscience.

But, does this wrap things up? Can it be that simple? Is Winner a moral hero and the public full of cowards, and we ought to provide her with the same support any hero deserves? Unfortunately, it can't be that quick. For one thing, what Thoreau means by "conscience" becomes much clearer when we put it in the context of his overall theoretical approach. Scholars like Nancy Rosenblum helpfully highlight the peculiarities of Thoreau's account of conscience, showing that he gives it a much larger role than most of us could accept for it. Moreover, even accepting Thoreau's approval of Winner isn't terribly helpful when it comes to the question of what *we*, as the public, have done wrong in failing to support her or failing to act like her.

Let Your Conscience Be Your Guide?

Conscience can seem like a catch-all for what each of us counts as good, but after looking to what Thoreau actually means by conscience, it's a poor guide to public ethics at least, especially given an alternative. Rosenblum describes Thoreau as a "militant" when it comes to conscience. She argues that we over-interpret Thoreau if we take him to be working in the same tradition as the liberty-focused

Founders, or even Paine or de Tocqueville. Thoreau, she offers, was no more interested in preserving liberal order than he was in preserving *any* type of order! Thoreau didn't recommended rebellion because it would preserve liberty. For Thoreau, rebellion is a path to self-actualization.

As Rosenblum so ably puts it, "Thoreau understood conscience in a fashion congenial to his romantic sensibility—as an exclusive, purely personal inner voice, a "genius"—and he portrayed conscientious action as a form of inspired self-expression, indeed, as a genial compulsion that is undeterred by obstacles and overcomes resistance." Uncom-promising might be the way to put it. And that translates into a kind of imposition, forcing our individual conscience, through our conscientious actions, onto those around us, albeit with the aim to challenge and transform others. For Rosenblum, this "aspiration to 'cast his whole influence' is arguably political; it is unmistakably intolerant and aggres-sive. Thoreau described conscientiousness in a militant's terms as a special form of aggression, and he identified personal purity with victory." I suspect many would agree with her.

When it comes to ethics, Rosenblum classifies Thoreau as an absolutist. So, it's clear now that, on Thoreau's accounting, the "cons" of releasing information about Russian attempts to influence our election become irrelevant. Winner herself becomes the only thing of relevance. Her bravery would be the light that was supposed to serve as a guide to the unconscious masses. She was personally inspired to take up a cause, did so, and in that case she can be relentless and uncompromising. Concerns for any external consistency or negative impact are beside the point if conscience is our guide.

Well, we can surely imagine some negative impacts if conscience gets in the wrong hands. Thoreau not only eliminates pragmatic concerns from political activism; he rids us of the ability to criticize any type of "inspired" extremism at all. And there's one final problem with Thoreau's take on Winner—he can't really make her a role model. Yes, she can inspire through her example, but in the end if you're not experiencing the inspiration, there's no way to muster it. Thoreau only worked on causes if he felt "continuous inspiration" toward them, a feeling that wasn't up to him. What can we really learn about the ethics of whistleblowing or leaking from this? Precious little.

I appreciate that Thoreau reminds us of our actual options. We certainly can release documents, we certainly can refuse to pay taxes. I think that why we *don't* do these things is something we should rehearse, just as if we were challenged by Thoreau to explain. But I also think that turning to a more rigorous ethical theory is a better way to put Winner's sacrifice in a useful context. We aren't meant to understand the inner workings of her conscience, but isn't there something far more easily communicated about what we she did, and why, available to us for assessing the ethics of leaking?

The Virtues of Conscience

Ethical theory doesn't always resonate with us on a first reading. It won't simply endorse what we already take ethics to be, and so working with it is part of a deliberate process. It's far more pleasing to sum up ethics in a few bromides or provocative lines, but in the end, we really need explanations of *how and why* when it comes to a problem like Russian interference in an election.

The right kind of ethical theory can also help us to retain Thoreau's reminder as to what's in our power, his ability to wake us up to actual options. And ethical theory can, as Thoreau also did, recognize that without being "enlivened" over an issue, all a theory offers is dry description of some good among countless others. To be motivated we must, as de Tocqueville insisted, have the actual "sublime desires" for what is right. We must feel it. The particular ethical theory that meets these considerations is virtue ethics, the approach first developed by the ancient Greeks like Plato, Aristotle, Epicurus, and the Stoics.

The boldest suggestion virtue ethics makes is that a level of understanding of what we are doing—a personal, non-technical, easily-elicited understanding—contributes to our own good, or virtuous, behavior. The standard of intelligibility is one matched to what regularly motivates us. We regularly represent to ourselves the norms we think we ought to follow, and virtue ethics asks us to include ethical and political norms in this set. It recognizes that even our political commitments can become vivid and be integrated into the rest of how we think about right and wrong.

As popular writer Ryan Holiday has come to appreciate, virtue ethics "cuts through the Gordian Knot of complex problems by zooming in on them at their smallest level: Not "How do I solve this enormous issue all by myself?" but "What can I do by myself, for myself, in response to what has happened?" Virtue ethics makes what to do about Winner a matter of *personal ethics* and not just politics.

How and why? By committing to various ethical norms that we attempt to articulate and test through practice (for example, lying is unacceptable in a public role), we develop confidence in the face of unethical behavior. We're able to recognize it, and we understand its costs. This means we have become personally invested in being ethical. A virtue ethicist won't think that just because it's a political fight decency is out the window, that wishing harm on others becomes acceptable, or that "all bets are off."

Nobody's Perfect

Traditional virtue ethics shouldn't be associated with lofty descriptions of complete virtue: it more realistically features *the role of norms* in typical behavior. That role is simply this: traditional virtue theorists expect us to identify and integrate good norms into our moral reasoning. When we do this, our behavior *becomes* virtuous, or ethical. When we fail to do this, our behavior is not virtuous (and may be vicious, or unethical). And, we needn't be conscious of the particular norms that guide us at any time; rather, they become internalized, matters of habit.

We might be wrong about what has motivated us. If asked, we might assert that a norm motivated our behavior even when it didn't. That's fine, normal, and to be expected and far better than just muddling ahead without any effort to articulate what's right. Stated norms identify and create the content with which we work and psychologically access when it comes to ethics. With this approach, even if one's behavior does not improve, the source of justification of good action (or policy) is personal and direct. Applying virtue ethics to our own take on the good of jailing and the good of law enforcement raises questions we don't otherwise find answered.

Ancient ethicists applied virtue ethics using what we can think of as a kind of questioning process. It's a method like that associated with Socrates, and would also be part of what Seneca describes as the "procedures of choice." The questions will also resemble those Cicero reports that the Stoic Panaetius invokes. The order in which these are taken does not matter, but at some point an agent must be encouraged to think through what they are claiming counts as good or ethical. To articulate a norm is one way to complete one's thoughts over an issue.

Another step involves distinguishing the norms we recommend from those we follow in our actual behavior. If there is a fit, then we would test these candidate norms in a manner that seems rather standard:

1. What is the good for which you are aiming?

2. Is it plausible that the behavior you are considering (various reactions to worries about Trump) matches the good you've just described? Can you defend the behavior in terms of the good you've identified?

3. Is the behavior you are considering unobjectionable even if roles were reversed? Is this what you would expect another to do?

4. Are you doing this for ethical reasons?

With this, we can put Winner's actions to the test. It seems a good candidate for the ethical norm she was operating under would be "I should risk my livelihood and freedom to share information that the public deserves."

Let's evaluate this norm. Does it identify some good? Yes. Does it fit with other things we endorse about citizenship? Yes. Is it capable of being maintained consistently with other commitments we expect people to hold? Yes. Does Winner's behavior actually get described adequately with this norm? As far as we know, yes. So, absent any arguments from security officials to the contrary, this might be enough to show us that Winner was ethically justified. Does it help us to recognize whether she is also deserving of our support?

Thoreau, as much as he mocked his neighbors for failing to have the courage of their convictions, was still the recipient of a paid bond. We think his neighbors admired his ethical stance and didn't want him to suffer for it. Does Winner deserve something similar? Virtue ethics can give us a way of answering. We can consider whether we too can endorse the norm she followed, and then we can be motivated to support her in the same way that we are motivated to recognize the norm's good. The complications of trying to honor all acts of conscience are uninvolved.

Instead, if due to her example we recognize a new norm and integrate it into our own commitments and moral psychology, we become better in a way we can recognize. It transforms our interests and we grow, no longer calculating only the good that can be demonstrated to be "utilitarian" or left to recognize nothing but "lust for power or fame or wealth." In other words, we develop beyond simple cost-benefit and self-interested norms and goals.

Everybody's a Winner

Virtue ethics reminds us that to do this requires a lot of deliberate work, sorting through potential norms and options available to us with an eye to doing the right thing. In this way, it gives Winner more credit than Thoreau does, who could merely point to Winner as someone with a strong conscience. Virtue ethics points out her bravery and her practical wisdom, should we find the norm that describes her behavior to be a good one.

Like Tom Paine used to do, a virtue ethicist would continually ask whether you could live with yourself if you accepted an unjust government. Virtue ethics would have you identify these limits. Virtue ethics would agree with thinkers like Vaclav Havel, who told us to assess politicians on the basis of the same standards of decency to which we hold others. A crude man is simply unethical, whether he votes for our causes or not. Like Thoreau, virtue ethics would never regard it as laughable that women marched against Trump's words about women. Lived commitments to honesty, decency, and dignity are "living in truth."

Imagine how much more we would understand about political values if we focused on completing this statement: "I should only pay taxes as long as the government . . ."

Imagine how much more we would understand ourselves.

15
E-Leaking as Civil Disobedience

Miquel Comas Oliver

Investigative journalism has a long tradition in our modern societies, and it has played a great role in the revelation of political scandals. For instance, we can recall the *Pentagon Papers*, analyzing the atrocities of American governments in Vietnam, which Daniel Ellsberg released to the press and the *New York Times* published in 1971.

Regarding the *Papers*, the philosopher Hannah Arendt (1906–1975) wrote an interesting article in 1972, but her focus wasn't the assessment of the leaking itself, as its title proves—"Lying in Politics." Her main interest was the great deal of lies within the documents. Warning us about a general prejudice in politics, that it's full of deception and Machiavellian behavior which teaches us the important difference between authenticity and truth in a disclosed file, she took it for granted that Ellsberg was totally right to reveal those documents.

We can sum up Arendt's assumptions to justify the leaking. First, the *Papers* didn't reveal anything that the public hadn't already known. Second, media really is and should be the fourth power of any democracy and, therefore, journalists have the right but also the duty to inform citizens about anything governments try to hide. And third, which is the most realistic and sad at the same time, the revelation of classified information is the only way to know the errors or misbehaviors that these documents reveal. That's so because, unfortunately, the elite who have restricted access to the secret data are far too lazy or busy to properly read the *Papers*. Hence, only open access to the general public would make them able to serve their original purpose: the self-critical analysis of policy-making.

Nevertheless, such a revelation would be very different today, because its forty-seven volumes wouldn't be manually copied or physically hidden to be leaked to the press. Let's take as an example the first well-known publication of WikiLeaks, the famous *War Diaries* from 2010, including the Iraq and Afghan War Logs. It contained more than 483,500 files. Can you imagine how many people, photocopiers, wheelbarrows, and vans would be necessary to transport all these? It would be practically impossible to manage to make it public. However, nowadays it only takes some digital space in the "cloud" and some memory sticks.

Was There Cryptology and Anonymity Before Computers? Obviously!

Encoding secrets has been a common practice in human history: when someone wants to send a message with important information, and it's necessary to avoid peepers, we typically write the data in a way that only those in the loop can read. That's the popular definition of a *cypher*. Cracking the cypher occurs when you've discovered the code that allows you to translate the information into a normal, human language.

Nevertheless, before the twentieth century, cryptography was useful only to politicians or the military. So, what happened in the last century that changed everything? The answer is computer engineering. With the processing power that computers began to exhibit, the whole system of rewriting the message to code or decipher it became impressively quick. This is how, during World War II, there was a big breakthrough: the cracking of the Nazi Enigma machine thanks to the calculus engine and Alan Turing's work team.

Another fundamental factor is that the coding doesn't depend anymore on the physical features of the object where the message is impressed, the "magical, invisible ink" or special box that's very difficult to open because of its complex mechanisms. It depends now on mathematical properties and relations, which are much safer and more stable. And finally, in the 1970s, some genius invented the "public key" or asymmetrical cryptography, a communication system that doesn't need to give the addressee the code to decipher the message, which had always been a practical problem insofar as there wasn't a secure information channel. With these variables, encryption became a very successful business, a powerful tool for security but also a great help for social movements.

Regarding anonymity, we simply need to remember that some of the great artists of all time hid their identities in order to be able to create their works of art. Many female writers used pseudonyms to publish. Even Banksy and other artists need to mask their identities. Moreover, this is also the only safe way to express your free opinion in the many countries where political pluralism doesn't exist and free expression is repressed.

Voilà! E-Leaking!

Given this historical combination of Information and Communication Technologies and anonymity via encryption, I propose a new word to describe *any* act of classified data disclosure that occurs this way today: *e-leaking*. This concept must be applied as much to anonymous actors on the network as to traditional mass media or investigative journalists. It applies, in other words, to any form of whistleblowing, because nowadays any disclosure of data must be *electronic*, not done by carrying around what would amount to several tons of paper documents.

The digital factor doesn't refer only to its lighter weight or its smaller dimensions. The most important thing is that, although full security is almost impossible, the current cryptological methods allow you to send and receive messages without leaving any trace of your identity. Even the receiver may not know the identity of the sender because the network is technically designed to remove it.

And that changes everything. There's no crime or persecution without a suspect, and that creates a certain impunity that helps explain the massive spread of e-leaking. As Julian Assange says, "courage is contagious," and while that may be true, it's only because you can feel relatively safe sending a confidential file to an encrypted mailbox through the Deep Web or by using tools such as Tor.

The phenomenon of e-leaking has a double dimension, though, captured by a second possible meaning of the letter "e" in the prefix: *ethical*. Here, e-leaking immerses us in a new field of discussion, not only technical but also ethical, political and moral. And it's here where philosophy has much to teach us about WikiLeaks and other forms of e-leaking. My bet is that these kinds of actions need to be understood as one possible subtype of "electronic civil disobedience."

Other forms could be the DDoS attacks—distributed denial-of-service attacks—practiced by groups like Anonymous, among many others. Or the free distribution of software or copyrighted content through file sharing programs peer-to-peer. Or hacking with a moral or political motive. My general assumption is that the adaptation of civil disobedience to the Internet would allow analyzing actions as more than just revealing secrets. And, obviously, the adequacy of e-leaking to the discourse of civil disobedience could be used to justify (or condemn) many more actors and social digital movements than just WikiLeaks, because, again, there are many other online platforms which perform e-leaking. Just one example is *Cryptome.org*, founded in 1996, at least ten years before WikiLeaks appeared.

So, Why Is WikiLeaks Different?

So far, we know that whistleblowing has been around for a long time. Encryption and anonymity have also been used for decades and even centuries. Moreover, there's been online leaking of secrets almost since the creation of the Web. But, WikiLeaks is something totally unique, because it's the perfect combination of all three: principled disclosure of classified documents and encryption techniques to such an extent that we can consider this website the true emergence of a new way of digital civil disobedience.

WikiLeaks marks a milestone, taking e-leaking to a totally new level of interest, impact and depth. In fact, *WikiLeaks is original because with it e-leaking has emerged as a new way of disobeying the law in the name of global justice*. WikiLeaks's revelations confirm that cyberspace is a new battlefield where power relationships aren't yet decided. That's terribly dangerous and one reason for the increasing interest in legal internationalization, because the State doesn't yet have control of everything on the Net.

Wait a Minute! Electronic Civil Disobedience, Seriously?

Yes. But, transnational cyberspace provides a new framework that challenges the old perspectives and justifications of illegal dissent. Therefore, philosophy becomes essential for understanding WikiLeaks but, *vice versa*, this project is also an opportunity to check our ideas regarding disobedience. To start with, e-leaking of covert data raises questions about different "validity conditions" that the principal Western political traditions, liberalism and republicanism, demand. In other words, these traditions demand that actors *justify* their disobedience by meeting certain requirements. Among others, based on their *non-violent* character, we should mention the following:

1. **Responsibility.** Disobeyers must accept any sanction or consequence of their illegal actions, as an evidence of their good will.

2. **Constitutional loyalty.** Disobeyers want to change or stop an unjust law or policy, but nevertheless they accept and respect the general legal system, having a profound commitment to it.

3. **Collectivity.** Only a group of individuals can perform an act of civil disobedience, not a single, isolated person.

4. **Publicity.** Disobeyers must inform of their intentions well in advance, warning the whole society and even police of the space and time in which they will act; this publicity gives greater credibility, value, and justice; and, tacitly or allegedly, the names of the actors are included.

At least, these were the *traditional* definitions of these conditions. But the rise of the Internet calls for a reconsideration because, as you can imagine, the application of anonymization algorithms *seems* to contradict publicity.

In fact, anonymity is one of the most crucial issues to consider. Unfortunately, most of the research on digital civil disobedience hasn't paid enough attention to it. Or worse, it rejects it. For instance, one of the first experts on the topic,

Stefan Wray, claimed that electronic civil disobedience should be performed openly, and its agents shouldn't hide their identities. This assumption makes it very difficult to include whistleblowing as civil disobedience, since informants are normally unknown. Something similar seems to be true of *collectivity, responsibility,* and *loyalty* as well, because current whistleblowers tend to be individuals, partially irresponsible, and not advocates of the judicial framework. In other words, they sometimes act alone and they don't turn themselves in to the authorities because they don't trust governments or the reliability of due process. This is certainly the case with both Julian Assange and Edward Snowden, "enclosed" in the Ecuadorian embassy and in Russia, respectively.

Finally, there's another reason for turning to the philosophy of civil disobedience. I find it a better approach to justifying e-leaking—at least, more acceptable than the arguments that WikiLeaks or Assange have given. They're based in an unspoken "fundamental norm," that it's legitimate to violate the applicable secret law if you reveal a crime or an immoral act in the process, which appeals to several different ideas and theories, not all of which are necessarily consistent, for example, liberalism, human rights, constitutionalism, utilitarianism, and even anarcho-capitalism. In my opinion, it's crucial to validate e-leaking based on a *participatory conception of democracy*, which is achieved by connecting it with the discourse of civil disobedience. So, how does a participatory conception of democracy apply to cyberspace?

Keystones about Offline Civil Disobedience

The best way to address the problem of civil disobedience is to think of it as a form of *obedience*, specifically obedience that must be morally and politically justified, and not disobedience at all. As English philosopher Thomas Hobbes (1588–1679) argued, the obedience of the people to norms is not a natural fact; therefore, any call for obedience should be justified. Hobbes thought that, before the formation of the state and of laws to govern it and regulate human behavior, each individual is totally free to do as they will, and the state and laws are willingly agreed to because such a condition of absolute freedom is a state of "war of all against all" in which human life is "solitary, poor, nasty, brutish, and short."

In fact, it's this very radicalized idea of freedom that, afterwards, leads liberalism to the defense of civil disobedience. Liberal scholars like John Rawls and Ronald Dworkin support the decision to flout a standard that violates their personal convictions or their most private sphere of autonomy. They even consider the tolerance of disobedience as an indicator of the democratic quality of a genuine liberal society. It's no surprise, then, that the definition of civil disobedience that prevails both academically and socially today is defined by liberalism: *a public, responsible, peaceful, conscious, and highly political act in favor of the public interest.* But, of course, these liberal thinkers severely restrict its practice, imposing specific requirements, such as having previously exhausted all *legal* avenues.

Changing stances a bit and pursuing a mix between liberalism and republicanism, the German philosopher Jürgen Habermas makes a strong distinction between *legality* and *legitimacy*. Habermas holds that current laws can only be presumed fair if, in their promulgation by majoritarian elections, this majority respected some "pre-legislative normative standards of legitimacy" constructed by intersubjective recognition (we collectively acknowledge them) through public deliberation. And, if the state is only based on the current law, then there isn't any absolutely requirable obedience. Only if justice and democracy exist can compliance with the laws be expected, but conditionally, never absolutely, since compliance is subject to a moral justice greater than mere law.

As long as Habermas admits the possibility of "legal offenses against legitimacy," that is, injustices *within* the law, he understands disobedience as a protest with mainly a symbolic character. Disobedience brings into being the very public opinion that molds policy-making, in order to change the immoralities embedded in the current laws. In that sense, acting illegally could be right, "out of moral insight" and, furthermore, the only instrument available against what he calls "institutionalized crime."

The previous doctrines have at least two interconnected problems. First, they tacitly involve only two actors: the disobedient against the national State. This is sometimes called "Westphalian myopia" or "methodological national-ism," a dogma that imposes national limitations on the discussion of justice or democracy. Its origin is The Peace of Westphalia (1648) that established a new political order in Europe, and it's still in force: sovereign states are forbidden to intervene in others' domestic affairs. This nationalistic structure incapacitates our ability to assess the actions of NGOs or cyber-activists at the transnational level. The second problem is that those conceptions presuppose the existence of a mature democratic system.

These two assumptions complicate understanding e-leaking as disobedience, because the current international framework (defined by a neoliberal, informational capi-talism) couldn't be deemed as a global rule of law. Hence, the previous acceptance of the general validity of all the legislation is an excessive and outdated request.

Highlights about Cyberspace

Based upon different authors, such as the hacker Margarita Padilla or the cyberfeminist Remedios Zafra, let me outline two ideas that describe the circumstances under which *any kind* of social action in cyberspace arises.

First, there are no *recognized democratic rights* in cyberspace . . . yet. Second, nevertheless (or precisely because of this fact), the Internet is a *new political sphere* for social movements, as a new "public-private sphere" that connects the denunciation of this digital precariousness with the claim for cyber-rights and Net neutrality.

As a result, "Internet struggles" have high costs and risks, both economically and judicially, even biologically, as the criminal process against Chelsea Manning teaches us: UN officials considered that Manning (who confessed to having revealed military secrets to WikiLeaks) received inhumane treatment or quasi-torture. These facts are already sufficient to make it legitimate to develop disobedient actions that don't meet the same requirements "offline" theories demanded, giving rise to an acceptable and even necessary anonymous cyberactivism.

Is E-Leaking a Rightful Form of Civil Disobediences? Absolutely!

Disclosing secrets is an inherently *symbolic act*. Chelsea Manning's main objective was to denounce the atrocities committed by the US in Iraq and Afghanistan in order to sway public opinion, promote political change, and avoid more innocent victims. WikiLeaks's website and Assange's public statements proclaim the same, vindicating the revelation of secrets as a "principled" action, morally and politically motivated.

Regarding the *peaceful* character of civil disobedience required by the traditional theories, I consider it met, although obviously our conclusions depend on the definition of violence we choose to apply. Suffice it to say, it's decisive that the US intention to identify e-leaking with cyber-terrorism should be rejected as based on an unacceptable analogy between the attack on the World Trade Center and a national cybersecurity violation, a "digital 9/11," *casually* justifying deep reforms like an Electronic Patriot Act.

Regarding *constitutional loyalty* and its public expression, *responsibility*, I'll just reiterate that the absence of fundamental rights in cyberspace, plus the democratic deficits of the world order, exempt us from these require-ments in the case of digital or electronic civil disobedience. The risk of disproportionate penalties, abuse and arbi-trariness on the Net makes e-leaking legitimate and even necessary as a compensatory device against this double defenselessness.

Besides, we can better justify the breach of the responsibility thanks to Hannah Arendt. She finds it absurd to demand from a disobedient person the same absolute sanctions compliance imposed on a criminal, precisely because disobedience shouldn't be treated as any ordinary crime. Arendt already distinguishes disobeyers from offenders because the former act publicly and without profit. It's possible to maintain that same distinction without having the obligation to accept *any* punishment, because this observance is only one of the several ways to meet a wider normative criterion: that the action be altruistic. Voluntarily accepting a sanction is an intuitive case of a non-selfish action, since the subject obeys something that supposedly is against his interest but in favor of the common good. On the contrary, the offender violates the law exclusively to benefit from this individual breach. However, it's wrong to reduce all forms of altruistic action to those undergoing punishment. In short, responsibility can be accepted in cyberspace, if no sanction endangers the personal integrity or there's a due legal process.

Only the leaking of secrets itself should be supported. Any other crime associated with it but independent of it should be punished. For example, if you commit murder or assault to obtain the information, such conduct should be punished. But the whistle-blower who already has legal access to the files shouldn't be punished for revealing them. Therefore, WikiLeaks primarily appeals to the conscience of all those who are in contact with embarrassing secrets without breaking the law. While the question of illegal access raises other issues, WikiLeaks only receives the data.

Regarding *publicity*, there's an analogous argument: knowledge of the people's identity isn't the criterion that makes actions correct. If someone steals something for personal enjoyment, this action will still be a crime despite having previously made his identity public. Fortunately, publicity isn't enough. But if an unknown person peacefully but illegally sits in a public square to protest about something *considered unjust by public opinion*, this action will remain as valid civil disobedience even though everyone ignores his identity.

So, publicity isn't necessary either. In fact, this way we discover the confusion between different conditions, *publicity* and *identity*. The experience of the Italian group *Tute Bianche* clarifies this. This anti-globalization movement fought in the streets wearing white overalls and hiding their faces. Their "invisibility" helped to protect them legally and to represent injustice that's systematically concealed from public scrutiny. This is already a good example of anonymous, offline civil disobedience. Its lesson: indispensable publicity is compatible with anonymity, because it doesn't demand the *identity* of the actors. But, it does entail the public character of the action itself, its justifications, and its effects. Consequently, e-leaking can be civil disobedience despite anonymity.

Regarding *collectivity*, once we have a group of people convinced about the injustice of a law or a policy, their illegal actions can be civil disobedience although they perform those acts individually, therefore meeting the other criterion. The collectivity requirement doesn't refer to the number of people who behave equally at the same space-time, but to the intersubjective, or mutual, agreement founding a concerted action, despite the possibility of an individual realization.

For example, if some people, involuntarily, blend into an illegal demonstration against something clearly unjust, they shouldn't be seen as disobeyers by an outside specta-tor, because, despite the same action, they don't share intentions. Thus, the important criterion is the previous understanding that subsequently can motivate an action, whether individual or collective. Hence, collectivity alludes to the necessary alliance between subjects, not its translation into action. So, a solitary hacker or a pro-fessional alone in his workplace can also be a civil disobeyer if they break the law out of collectively justified reasons.

Eighth Dump

Open Secrets

16
Plugging the Leak in the Good Citizen Ship

BRAD PATTY

Wikileaks is frequently claimed to be a tool of Russian intelligence. While WikiLeaks denies this, and the truth of the claim is currently unknowable, the charge that they are a sort of enemy action is a general problem for the credibility of WikiLeaks (as well as for that of any similar efforts). This is true not only in the case of the United States and Russia, but potentially for similar projects between any two governments.

This raises a pair of crucial questions. First, to what degree is engaging in a potential enemy action compatible with good citizenship? Second, what are the ethical limits of making use of an enemy information operation for your own purposes?

Lessons from the Front

Two famous recent cases of Americans leaking to the Russians, one through WikiLeaks's alleged connections and the other through direct contact with the Russian government and via similar leak-oriented international journalism, are those of Chelsea Manning and Edward Snowden.

Looking at the ethical behaviors each took *before* the leaks, as well as citizen reaction to those leaks, we can extract the relevant ethical principles and apply them to the similar case of Donald Trump, Jr., who apparently agreed to consider information provided by the Russian government, aimed at influencing American politics in the presidential election of 2016. This serves as a test against the danger of being swayed by partisanship. While many who support Snowden also support Manning, almost no one who supports Snowden also supports Trump.

Finding principles that apply to *all three cases* suggests that the principles themselves are nonpartisan and disinterested, as far as possible. I believe that these three cases show that there are ethical principles that can control the damage done by hostile intelligence sufficiently that working with a hostile organization is consonant with good citizenship, though only in cases where the information is of great moment to the health of the nation of which one is a citizen.

Two categories of ethical behavior bookend the involvement of hostile intelligence. First, behaviors that *precede* the involvement of hostile intelligence. And second, behaviors that *follow* such involvement. The cases of Manning and Snowden differ significantly in the first category. This is where questions of motive come into play. Motive is important because it's the principle of our action, the *reason* on the basis of which we act. It's what *moves* us to act. For example, while stealing classified information for the public good might be considered morally justified because our motive is to serve the public good, stealing classified information in order to blackmail someone wouldn't. So, motive must be considered as far as it can be.

Manning's motivation appears to have been chiefly personal, a passionate sense of victimhood seeking an outlet for revenge. Snowden, by contrast, seems to have been motivated chiefly by ethical alarm at what he discovered his government was doing. The external and public character of their decisions about what and how to leak reinforces this impression of their internal motives. Manning leaked quite indiscriminately, not even reviewing the information to have some sense of what was being passed on to WikiLeaks. Snowden appears to have exercised some care to leak selectively only that information that would shed light on the programs he found alarming.

A Person of Principles?

Care in discrimination, however, doesn't change the fact that both leaks were acts of theft *and* oath-breaking, since the information was *owned* by the US government, and both Manning and Snowden had sworn oaths to keep the secrets they wound up leaking.

Manning, in fact, had *two* oaths to keep, the oath to protect secrets and the oath of enlistment. In treating this as a question of good citizenship, I'm setting aside the question of betrayal of fellow servicemembers. That's not because I view the question as unimportant—quite the opposite—but because here I'm looking at the compatibility of Wikileaks with good citizenship rather than compatibility with military honor.

Nevertheless, Snowden's discrimination is significant because it limits the exposure of secrets to a narrow class judged to raise substantial ethical and moral issues. But, how substantial do these issues need to be to justify both theft and oath-breaking?

American classification is always based on the grounds that release of the information could cause at least significant harm to America's national security. Documents classified as "secret" must be established to be capable of causing "grave harm" to American national security; "top secret" documents must be shown to be capable of causing "*exceptionally* grave harm." So, there's a degree of proportionality that we can assess with respect to the kind of information released. Specifically, the good to be obtained by bringing the information to the American public's awareness for public debate must equal or exceed the harm expected by its release.

It might look as if things are worse for Snowden than they are for Manning, given that Snowden leaked "top secret" documents exposing programs that were classified at the highest levels, whereas Manning only had access to "secret" documents that were all considered less damaging to national security. However, the indiscriminate leaking of documents means that Manning didn't even attempt to make the calculation of proportionality. Snowden appears to have done so and to have been satisfied that the harm caused by the exposure of these programs was proportionate to the good to be done by exposing American spying activities to the citizenry. This gives us our first two principles in the first category of behaviors that precede the leak. First, the leak must be *discriminate*. And second, it must be *proportionate*.

A third principle is that leaking information should not be *treasonous*. Treason is an act of war against one's own government, or otherwise rendering "aid and comfort" to *enemies*—by which I mean, and believe the statute to mean, those who are at war with one's own government. Snowden comes off better here as well. The Russian government is certainly a competitor state with the United States, and these two states are at times hostile to one another's interests. But Russia wasn't an enemy of the United States, since no war existed (nor was one contemplated) at the time of Snowden's decision to work with the Russians.

Manning, by contrast, leaked information knowing that

it would aid and comfort actual enemies—in the form especially of Al Qaeda in Iraq—with whom the United States was indeed at war. Treason is obviously incompatible with good citizenship, and this difference between "sometimes hostile" and "actual enemy at war against you" is significant.

The final principle in the first category is that the information should be *true*. In a sense, this is part of the proportionality criterion, as there would be no sense in suffering the harm to be caused by revelation of the secret if there was no truth to expose to the citizenry. However, the mere fact that a classified document contains information doesn't guarantee that information's truthfulness. Before causing the harms associated with the revelation of secrets, you have a duty to ensure that there's indeed a good to be had. Ascertaining the truth is therefore a responsibility of the leaker.

After the Fact

So much for the first category. The second category concerns what follows the leak. The first principle in this second category is that you should *submit to the judgment of your peers*. Here, Snowden has been lacking. Rather than turning himself in to face trial, he fled to Russia, where he would be subject to additional pressures to give up intelligence in an indiscriminate and disproportionate manner.

Manning was captured and appears to have exercised no will to be judged by other Americans. Rather, Manning continued to steal and transmit as long as possible. Both are failures on this score and, although Manning received a commutation (as well as a very generous set of charges, not including treason), both are to be faulted. You can't unilaterally set aside the judgment that the secrets being leaked are properly kept secret, because the government that makes this decision was elected by the citizenry as a whole or appointed by those who were. In other words, the actions of the government in keeping this information secret are ostensibly actions in accordance with the will of the people.

In Snowden's case, he believed that the government wasn't acting in a way the people would approve of, and he wanted to ensure public debate about whether or not these sorts of programs were really in accord with the popular will. That may be a fair judgment in many cases. But, in order to test that, you must submit your individual judgment to the review of the citizenry. The most obvious way to do that is to submit to the judgment of a jury of your peers.

Such a test is especially relevant in Snowden's case. Manning failed every single test of good citizenship in this regard, but Snowden may not have. It could prove, on examination, that he was a Russian agent all along; or, it could prove he gave away more than was proportionate. So, to make any final decision about whether his conduct was consistent with good citizenship, it's necessary to have an open hearing and present the facts for judgment by the citizens.

Full Disclosure

The second principle, related to the first, is that one must make clear to the public the presence of the hostile foreign organization. One of the things the public needs is to be able to judge what interests the hostile power is pursuing by pushing this information into the American public debate. While it may not be possible to disentangle completely the foreign interests from the good citizen interests that led the leaker to make the leak, the public can do as much as possible if and only if they know that it's an issue to be considered.

In addition to the duties that the leaker himself may have, other citizens who are considering and debating this information also have duties in the second category. It might seem as if, being loyal citizens, they ought simply not to look at leaked secrets or forward a public debate about them. After all, their government classified those secrets for reasons that are presumably valid exercises of the public trust. Yet, the fact is that government officials don't always act in accord with the public trust.

The debate subsequent to Snowden's leaks showed that Snowden's judgment about the American people was correct: they were indeed deeply disturbed by his revelations about the degree of NSA and other activity. Though a number of whistleblowing processes exist within the government and through various channels, there may be cases like this one in which there's simply no other way to bring the information forward. No military chain of command is going to release such information. No inspector general is going to tell the public about it. Members of Congress may not even have the clearance to be told about the programs, not even if they know to ask about them.

When a direct appeal to the public is made through a leak of this kind, the American people have to evaluate the information's worth. Loyalty to the American project includes making sure that the government doesn't depart from the ideals and values underlying that project. The same holds for citizens of other nations in similar circumstances.

Due Diligence

When evaluating the information that has fallen into their hands, citizens have a duty of *due diligence*. Of course, if the information is classified, ordinary citizens won't be able simply to check to see if the information is accurate. However, there will likely be details that citizens *can* check, and these should be verified as far as possible. If the story checks out insofar as it's possible to check it, then it may be worth taking seriously.

This is an important duty given that Russian propaganda efforts, particularly in eastern Europe, are often wildly untrue (as are many other propaganda efforts). WikiLeaks itself so far has a strong track record of leaking true information from valid documents. Nevertheless, it's not consonant with good citizenship to believe a story simply because it was leaked from classified documents. Nor can we rely on the reputation of an outlet that's known to be hostile to your government and still be a good citizen. You must be diligent.

These principles in the second category are unified by the aim of having a clear, public debate among citizens since this is the potentially acceptable justification for the act of oath-breaking and theft. The act can only be justified, that is, if its aim is to bring something crucial forward to the citizenry for their action. Citizens should therefore have that debate and take appropriate action, and they should have the debate in fair, public, and honest ways. When they determine that the secrets really should have been kept, they should punish the oath-breaking and theft as the serious matters they are.

There may, however, be some cases in which they affirm that the oathbreaker has been a good citizen, that they acted appropriately. They may decide that the government was keeping a secret that it shouldn't have been. Given that the citizenry as a whole is the sovereign in a republican or democratic form of government, the citizenry has every right to over-rule the mere government and make that determination. The citizenry can say that it, and not the government, was, as sovereign, the proper owner of information being kept secret, and thus that the secret wasn't *stolen* but rather *returned*.

The Trump Card

There is, then, a narrow path for the ethical use of a hostile intermediary to bypass government channels in order to bring secret information forward for public debate. This is consonant with good citizenship if and only if there's considerable ethically valid behavior on both sides of the involvement of the hostile intermediary. Nevertheless, however narrow, such a path does exist. So, having worked out all of these principles and determined that there is a path, let's test them by applying them to the similar case of Donald Trump, Jr., who by his own admission took a meeting with a Russian national under the belief that she was bringing him information from the Russian government that could help sway an American election. What do these principles tell us about this case?

First, there are some significant differences. One such difference is that the information in question wasn't stolen. The whole set of questions around the morality of stealing information therefore doesn't apply. Russian intelligence belongs to Russia in the same way that the intelligence leaked by Manning and Snowden belongs to America, and that intelligence is thus Russia's to give away if they choose. Likewise, neither Donald Trump, Jr., nor the Russian agent (if she was an agent) was breaking an oath. (I assume Trump has no sworn oath to protect Russian secrets, and the Russian agent would have been acting on orders.) An American collecting Russian secrets to pass to Americans isn't like an American stealing American secrets to pass to Russia. Thus, those moral concerns are also not relevant.

There is, however, an additional concern that information coming from the Russian government might be infected with propaganda falsehoods. Should Trump have looked at information coming from the Russian government at all, given the risk of infecting the public debate with Russian propaganda?

This is analogous to the principles of proportionality and due diligence in the WikiLeaks cases. Looking at the information as someone deciding whether or not to introduce it into the public debate, we must be proportionate, balancing the risk of infection by falsehoods with the significance of the information if it turns out to be true. It wouldn't do to introduce information that claimed to prove something that was merely tawdry, for example. Even if true, it wouldn't be of legitimate public interest to a degree adequate to justify the risk of infection. The claimed information would need to be significant, perhaps demonstrating a serious crime or a serious incapacity for office.

By the same token, before introducing the information, we would have to conduct due diligence to ensure as far as possible that it's accurate. If it doesn't appear to be true, then it shouldn't be brought forward—leaked, as it were, into the public debate. The hostile intelligence service is attempting to gain something by passing this information to you; in order to justify passing that information forward on the grounds of good citizenship, you have to be convinced that it's both true and proportionate.

Motive as a principle is directly relevant here. Trump's motive would naturally be suspect: the benefit to his family would have been impossible for him to disentangle from the advantage to the country of any public debate. Does that mean that any such use would be forbidden, given his motive problems? Not necessarily. It might be possible, if he could find a disinterested third party, to pass it to them and promise to accept their judgment on whether or not the information should be released. Still, that's probably only a theoretical possibility, since there are very few who are disinterested in the question of the choice of the next American president. So, it may be that the best that can be done is transparency, allowing the public to judge his (at best) mixed motives.

In actuality, there was no Russian intelligence for Trump to pass on. But if there had been, and if he had chosen to pass it, he would have also been subject to the duty of transparency about its source. His fellow citizens would have needed to know that the source of the information was a sometimes-hostile foreign power with an agenda of its own. Only in that way could such citizens filter for the hostile motives as well as possible, limiting the successful manipulation by the Russians.

This transparency serves an additional function. Professional intelligence officers in clandestine service are trained manipulators, and you must assume you're being manipulated in your meetings with them. However, such manipulation is by its nature *targeted*. It targets the individual to be manipulated, his or her particular hopes, dreams, politics, aspirations, and so forth. By bringing the information to the general consideration of the citizenry as a whole, much of that targeting is disabled. The whole citizenry can therefore judge the information better than could the original individual, as long as they have been forthrightly informed that this is coming from foreign intelligence.

And of course, having admitted the source of the information, Trump would have had to subject himself to the judgment of his peers as to the propriety of his actions. There's some debate about whether Trump will face a jury trial over his meeting, which (should it occur) would be one form of doing so. In the hypothetical case in which he had received and used Russian information, his clarity about its source would also have allowed his fellow citizens to judge his actions via the election itself.

Pitfalls on the Path

The hypothetical only shows that there's a *narrow* path to the ethical use of information received from a hostile intelligence service. It doesn't prove that Trump would have, in fact, stayed on that path. There are many ways to go wrong on it. He could have been disproportionate, forwarding irrelevant but tawdry information that would have been merely scandalous rather than necessary to bring to the public's attention. He could have failed to do due diligence, or—having discovered that the information was likely false in the course of his due diligence—passed on what he knew or strongly suspected to be a lie.

He could have hidden the source, forcing the American people not to take account of what would have then been a hidden Russian agenda in the background of the debate. In that way, too, he could have avoided subjecting himself to the judgment of his peers as to whether or not his action was proper. Still, and perhaps surprisingly, the question of his good citizenship doesn't turn on the fact that he was communicating with a hostile foreign intelligence service. As with the WikiLeaks cases, there's a narrow path for good citizens here.

Having applied these principles, we can say that working with a group like WikiLeaks can be an exercise of good citizenship in spite of the danger that it's a front for Russian intelligence. Indeed, even working with Russian intelligence can be an exercise of good citizenship for an American, at least in theory.

In practice, much virtuous and ethical behavior is demanded of the good citizen on each side of the act involving the hostile foreign power. It may be that few if any are of strong enough character to pull it off. But, it's at least possible, when it's done in the interest of restoring the sovereignty of the people over questions of especial moment.

And that goes for all nations, not just the United States.

17
Selfless Whistleblowing and Selfish Leaking

JOSHUA HAUTALA AND ADAM BARKMAN

On November 8th 2016, the unexpected happened. Hillary Rodham Clinton lost the US presidential election.

Her rival, Donald Trump, dominated the Electoral College vote, shocking not only many in America, but also the world. His election was truly revolutionary in the world of politics. Numerous and varied factors played a role in Trump's victory, unhappiness with the status quo among working, middle-class voters being one of them.

Clinton, on the other hand, in her book *What Happened*, blamed her loss on such factors as misogyny, mainstream news, Bernie Sanders, the FBI, James Comey, her campaign, women voters, Russia, and most importantly, the ongoing email scandal and related Democratic National Committee (DNC) leaks.

Of these factors, two are most relevant to the subject of WikiLeaks: the leaks of DNC emails via WikiLeaks, and the leak of several memos by former FBI director James Comey. One of these is most likely the result of whistleblowing by an individual or individuals within the DNC. The other was a leak to the media of seven memos written by James Comey (via a personal friend) of which four purportedly contained classified information.

The definition of whistleblowing has changed. In the past, a person releasing information that was deemed internal to a company or organization (business or political) was viewed primarily as an "informant." As often as not, this held a negative connotation, as did the term "whistleblower." The whistleblower was seen as "blowing the whistle" on those to whom he was expected to show loyalty.

In more recent writing, however, the status of the whistleblower has been elevated to something more akin to that of a hero, as someone who resists corruption in government, business or any other organization. A whistle-blower, much like an old-school reporter like Lois Lane and Clark Kent, serves the greater good by releasing information to the public. Society as a whole benefits, while often the person or organization that's revealed in this way suffers financial and other losses. If there's illegality involved, then jail time and fines are common results.

Going with the more recent definition of a whistle-blower, we introduce the term "leaker" as a moral opposite. A leaker is someone who gives out proprietary information (whether in business or politics) for personal—primarily selfish—reasons, without regard for any negative social or larger group impact. The actions of a "leaker," however, and not just those of a "whistleblower," may have an overall positive impact in some way. To better keep the two distinct, we consider personal motivation as the primary distinguishing factor between a selfless whistleblower and a selfish leaker.

So, Are You Moral or Not?

The question of right and wrong can be either simple or complex depending on your belief system. In order to analyze the difference between a moral decision (one with an unselfish motive) and an immoral one (which has a selfish motive), there must be some basis used as a "moral compass."

The authors Patrick Sullivan and Ola Ngau, surveying recent writing on business ethics, commented that moral analysis, in general, has been lacking. Instead, this aspect of philosophy has tended to lead to division and "emotionally charged extremes." This is not unlike the situation in American politics today. We often hear about the "left" and "right" viewpoints when it comes to things like politics, religion, family values and morals in general. The extreme polarization of moral sides has become the norm. While it often begins as a political argument, the debate is often rooted in two different belief systems. This leads to inevitable divisions.

For our part, we assert that a moral judgment and a primordial moral responsibility are implied when we talk about right and wrong. Therefore, in order to proceed, we must take as understood that there exists a funda-mental moral code or "natural law"—a moral law or code that we all inherently share: Plato's Good, the Stoics' Natura, Zoroaster's Asha, the Hindu Rta, the Egyptian Ma'at, Confucius's Propriety, Aquinas's Natural Law, Kant's Categorical Imperative, and so on. Certainly, different cultures and situations provide different inferences from this code, but all cultures do—consciously or unconsciously— share some basic universal moral beliefs.

The examples this chapter uses to help define selfless whistleblowing in contrast to selfish leaking, therefore, assume that the distinction between what's considered "good" and "bad" behavior is, at its most fundamental level at least, universally understandable—what's good or right or just is what treats persons or things according to what they are, whereas what's bad or wrong or unjust treats persons or things with little to no regard for what they are.

One further assumption here is that the self isn't the most important thing in the cosmos and, therefore, an action that elevates the self above everyone and everything else regardless of any other considerations is unjust and wrong. More specifically, an action that's intended to benefit others—which is to say, an action that gives proper regard to others—is a just, good, or moral action, whereas an action that's intended primarily to benefit the self over and against equal or greater considerations is a bad, unjust, or immoral action. And this lies at the heart of the distinction between just whistleblowing and unjust leaking.

Show and Tell

Imagine you are a senior division manager of a major pharmaceutical company, personal friends with the company's CEO, and on the fast track for promotion. Life sounds good, right? Well, it is for you; but at a recent meeting, you've discovered that the latest miracle drug your company has come up with is a little *too* good. In fact, your VP of marketing insisted, with the CEO's agreement, the company sell a weakened form of the drug to increase profit margins. After all, your company has stockholders to please. Users of the drug will see a lessened benefit and, as a result, they will be forced to purchase more of the drug for a similar outcome.

Knowing that this practice will put the drug out of the financial reach of many sick people, what do you do? A whistleblower, by our definition, will do the selfless thing. In this example, trying to convince the CEO not to follow the given advice might be the first step. If that doesn't work, then the decision whether to risk one's job by exposing the situation becomes a moral choice. If you choose to do so, this would, by our definition, be considered the act of a whistleblower. The act is a selfless one taken to benefit others, with the real possibility of negative consequences for yourself. The fact that you might be seen as a "hero" is not part of your motivation.

Imagine that the same situation occurs, but it just so happens that you're not personal friends with the CEO, and you're let go due to company downsizing. You happen to be privy to the fact that the company will be selling a diluted form of the new drug. With evidence you have taken with you from the company, you approach a news station to expose the CEO and VP of marketing as callous, profit-seeking individuals. While the positive outcome may be the same (the company doesn't sell the diluted drug), the motivation is primarily one of revenge aimed at damaging the CEO and VP of marketing. This would be a classic example of leaking. The leaker, in this case, has no job to lose and as a further bonus has the possibility of being seen as a "hero." The leaker does it for himself, motivated by selfish reasons, whereas the whistleblower does it in spite of the harm it could cause him.

You Will Know Them by Their Fruits

But how do we truly determine motivation? No one is a mind reader, but we suggest that motivation can, in *most* cases, be determined by the consequences of the action for the person who "spills the beans."

Most examples in modern literature see whistleblowing as a selfless act that's done to benefit society as a whole in some way. It may be the case of exposing a corrupt business practice that puts society at risk or a corrupt aspect of government. In many cases of this type of whistleblowing, the consequences are negative for the whistleblower, even resulting in death, though these cause and effect relationships can be difficult to prove.

The controversy surrounding the death of Seth Rich and his connection to the DNC is a case in point. Julian Assange of WikiLeaks has very strongly implied that Seth Rich was the leaker in the DNC case. He has even offered a reward for the capture of his killers, which is possibly telling. The authorities hypothesize that it was a robbery; however, nothing was stolen.

On the other hand, very little is written about leakers. These are individuals who leak information in order to gain personal advantage or benefit. The consequences of this type of leaking are by their nature hurtful towards a group or individual in some way. We think that most of the time there will be little social benefit from leaking, though it's acknowledged that this may be a secondary result. The motivation of the leaker is selfish in nature, and so any beneficial result is of secondary importance to them.

Anonymous tip lines are sometimes set up by governments or organizations as a way to protect whistleblowers. This is helpful in many cases; however, a whistleblower will persevere regardless of this protection. A leaker though, by definition and based on the selfish nature of their leaking, will wish to avoid negative consequences. An anonymous tip line, therefore, is an ideal tool for such an individual to use. Another method to maintain anonymity is to leak via a trusted third party. The primary difference is that an unselfish whistleblower will "blow the whistle" even if such avenues are not available, whereas a leaker will likely not. The whistleblower has altruistic motivations, whereas the leaker seeks a primary outcome that is for personal benefit, often (though admittedly not always) at the expense of others.

The Difference Between Assange and Comey

Julian Assange, as the founder of WikiLeaks, has overseen, since 2006, the release of an enormous amount of information of great importance. This information has revealed, for example, unlawful surveillance methods that the US government and its various intelligence agencies have used on its own citizens. In many cases, these governmental practices have had extremely negative effects on private citizens.

Assange's stated goal has been to reveal the truth behind these government practices and let society make its own judgments. His actions, however, have had tremendous negative personal consequences, and despite his stated neutrality, it's obvious from the nature of the information released that his motivations are unselfish in nature. He gains little personally from his actions. Further, he has stated that he would never release any information that would put lives at risk.

In 2012, Julian Assange was forced to take asylum in the Ecuadorian embassy in London due to an unsubstantiated claim of sexual harassment. Government bodies have sought his extradition on very dubious legal grounds. It's very likely that Assange would face severe consequences were he taken into custody by any of these governmental bodies. He has lived in a single room for the past six years, separated from his own family. It's difficult to imagine a more severe consequence of whistleblowing.

The (likely) unselfish nature of Assange's actions needs to be assessed based on outcomes and consequences. The consequences he has faced are obviously negative, the information he has released has led to the positive outcome of government corruption being exposed. We, therefore, will define his actions as more-than-likely unselfish in nature, with the caveat that we still have not learned to read minds and motivations can be unclear at the best of times.

A prime example of the work of WikiLeaks is the release of emails that were taken from the server of the Democratic National Committee (DNC). The release of these emails exposed potential corruption within the DNC and individuals associated with it. Indeed, the head of the DNC was fired after these emails were released to the public. Others within the DNC have been implicated in corruption, and the information has led to further investigation. The premise of Russian interference in the election has been brought into question. Rep. Dana Rohrabacher interviewed Julian Assange and briefed President Trump on this meeting. The story itself is ongoing, but Julian Assange is still locked away in exile.

On the other hand, James Comey, who was the former director of the FBI, has in recent times leaked several personal memos. He did this via a third party and has suffered no public consequences. However, the leaked memos (one in particular) have resulted in the appointment of a special prosecutor who searched diligently to find wrongdoing on the part of Trump and his associates. This examination has even led to the appointment of a Grand Jury. Paul Manafort (a previous Trump campaign associate) had his home raided in search of incriminating evidence, all this as a result of Comey's leaking.

The motivation behind the leaking of this particular memo by Comey, therefore, has resulted directly in the investigation of the man who fired him. This then is likely a prime example of selfish leaking in order to seek retaliation against an individual. Comey's motivation doesn't seem primarily motivated by selflessness. Comey is free to pursue his future career and life without consequences for his actions, whereas Assange is not free and may never truly be free.

Isn't It Ironic?

James Comey has said that our obligation is "to refuse to let bad win, to refuse to let evil hold the field." While we certainly agree with Comey here, we have to ask whether there isn't some irony to his claim. Comey has come out of his situation quite well—as most who attack President Trump in the mainstream media do—and it's hard not to see Comey as an agent of "evil" on this particular field.

Julian Assange, on the other hand, tells us that "Capable, generous men do not create victims, they nurture victims." James Comey has sought to create victims. Julian Assange via WikiLeaks has, it appears, sought to reveal those who create victims and, in the process, has become a victim himself.

18
Kill Switch Engage

CHRISTIAN COTTON

> There is a view that one should never be permitted to be criticized for being even possibly in the future engaged in a contributory act that might be immoral, and that that type of arse-covering is more important than actually saving people's lives. That it is better to let a thousand people die than risk going to save them and possibly running over someone on the way. And that is something that I find to be philosophically repugnant.
>
> —JULIAN ASSANGE, in the movie *WikiLeaks: Secrets and Lies*

There you are, sitting at your computer, one click away from dropping a trove of classified documents that exposes the corruption, deception, and illicit behavior of some of the most powerful institutions in the world.

If you click that button, the information will become available to anyone with access to the Internet, and the truth will be set free. If you don't click the button, the truth of those immoral actions will remain unknown and those powerful institutions will continue their corruption and deception unpunished. Don't you have a moral obligation to at least give justice the *chance* of being served? It's an obvious question, and most would likely say yes.

But, hang on.

What if, by clicking the button and releasing all that information, you could be putting a lot of innocent people in harm's way? It's a noble thing to want corruption and injustice exposed, but is it worth the risk of endangering the well-being of innocent people, who may suffer as a result? If we *know* it will cause harm, then we have reason *not* to click the button; but, if we only know that harm is *possible*, then we face a more challenging decision given the kind of information that will be brought to light if we choose to click the button. Do we have a moral obligation in this case to release the documents?

It's a fundamental point of controversy about WikiLeaks that by releasing the kinds of sensitive information it's famous for, it exposes many innocent lives to danger through no fault of their own. If we consider the enormous information dumps made by Chelsea Manning and Edward Snowden as just two examples among many, the worry becomes more acute: in attempting to "do the right thing" to expose corruption or deception by revealing the truth, such actions place in the way of direct harm individuals who themselves are neither complicit nor directly involved in that corruption or deception. But, this is morally objectionable, right?

On the other hand, isn't *not* releasing these kinds of information itself morally objectionable, not least because failure to do so is corrosive to the very foundations of a free society? A government in the shadows is antithetical to transparency and accountability, thus restricting the power of the people to what the government *chooses* to acknowledge.

Is there a correct moral response to the question of leaking, whistle-blowing, secrecy, and transparency? You probably find yourself leaning one way or the other, right? Perhaps there *is* a correct response, but before we can adequately address that problem, it's helpful to understand a bit about the *kind* of dispute that's going on here. If we can better understand where the two opposed positions are coming *from*, then we just might be able to avoid unnecessary confusion and disagreement and be better able to focus on where to *go* in solving the problem. Let's call it the WikiLeaking Problem.

This problem is reminiscent of another, more famous, philosophical problem called the Trolley Problem. What if we look at the WikiLeaking Problem as a particular case of the Trolley Problem and try to draw out the crux of the disagreement, even if we find that it leaves us in an awkward position regarding a solution?

The Trolley Problem

The trolley problem is a thought experiment in ethics developed by philosopher Philippa Foot in her 1967 article, "The Problem of Abortion and the Doctrine of Double Effect." Foot presents the following scenario with three similar cases, one of which is the source for the trolley problem:

> Suppose that a judge or magistrate is faced with rioters demanding that a culprit be found for a certain crime and threatening otherwise to take their own bloody revenge on a particular section of the community. The real culprit being unknown, the judge sees himself as able to prevent the bloodshed only by framing some innocent person and having him executed. So, by having an innocent person executed, the judge can save several innocent lives.
>
> Beside this example is placed another in which a pilot whose airplane is about to crash is deciding whether to steer from a more to a less inhabited area. To make the parallel as close as possible it may rather be supposed that he is the driver of a runaway tram which he can only steer from one narrow track on to another; five men are working on one track and one man on the other; anyone on the track he enters is bound to be killed. In the case of the riots the mob has five hostages, so that in both examples the exchange is supposed to be one man's life for the lives of five.

Foot herself didn't flesh out the trolley problem as a distinct moral quandary. But if we expand on her case, as many have done in the years since 1967, the general form of the problem looks like this:

> There's a runaway trolley barreling down a set of tracks. Ahead, on the tracks, there are five people tied up, unable to move out of the way. The trolley is headed straight for them. You happen to be

standing some distance off in the trolley yard, next to a lever that controls the tracks. If you pull this lever, the trolley will switch to a different set of tracks, sparing the lives of the five people. However, you notice that on the side track there's one person tied up, unable to move out of the way. Diverting the trolley will result in the death of this one person. Would you pull the lever or not?

Can I say that, in pulling the lever, I don't *intend* the death of the single individual who will surely die as a result of my action? (Or will he surely die? More on the real-world application of this thought experiment in a bit.) What if I intend to save lives instead? This way of thinking is directly related to a philosophical doctrine known as Double Effect. (For a closer look at double effect, see Chapter 4).

The Trolley Problem leaves us with the question, "Can it be morally justified to *kill* one innocent person *in order to save* five innocent people?" By analogy, the WikiLeaking Problem leaves us with the question, "Can it be morally justified to put the lives of innocent people in danger in order to expose the immoral actions of others, in this case powerful governments that often act with a sense of moral impunity?"

The Fat Man

To further test individuals' moral psychology, the trolley problem has been modified in several ways. Now, we're not talking about the very popular trolley problem memes you might encounter on Facebook which, while quite creative and often very amusing, fundamentally misconstrue the basis of the trolley problem as a test of moral psychology. (You can check them out at <www.facebook.com/TrolleyProblem Memes>.)

In perhaps the most well-known modified version of the problem, you're confronted with a choice that puts you in much more intimate contact with the individual who will die as a result of your actions should you choose to intervene on behalf of the five people tied to the track. Whereas in the original scenario, you pulled a lever (or not) which resulted in a person far down the track dying, in this scenario you must choose whether or not to push a fat man off a bridge that runs over the trolly track on which the five folks are tied. If you push the fat man over, he'll land on the track, stopping the trolley from reaching the others. Would you push the fat man off the bridge?

Most would say no, of course. After all, *that* would be killing. And yet, many of those same people would pull the lever in order to save the five people tied to the tracks. But, isn't that *also* killing? Maybe not, we might tell ourselves. That one individual may die as a result of our action, but we won't really have killed them. And yet, it's nevertheless true that, in both scenarios, someone dies as a result of our action.

It hardly seems we can deny that. Still, many will choose differently in the two cases. Some have suggested that the explanation for this is that we perceive a distinction between *killing* and *letting die*. In the fat man scenario, we killed him by pushing him off the bridge. But, in the lever scenario, pulling the lever isn't a direct cause of death the way pushing the fat man is. There's a kind of *moral distance*. We *feel* very differently in the two scenarios, based on how *close* we are in the causal chain.

Think about another, analogous, set of scenarios. In a time of war, you are faced with the decision to pull the trigger or not to neutralize an enemy combatant. Like the fat man scenario, this implicates you more closely than an equally analogous scenario to pulling the lever in which, from a distance, you're faced with a choice to push a button that will fire a shot from an overhead drone. Or, perhaps even more aptly analogous, you're the commanding officer who signs off on the execution of an enemy combatant—in other words, you give the "kill command" but don't actually pull the trigger . . . or push the fat man.

Now, if the options are kill or be killed, we already have a deeply held moral intuition and evolutionarily sophisticated internal drive to defend ourselves. So, from the practical as well as the moral standpoint, such cases aren't controversial or even problematic. Of course, we can still choose to place ourselves in harm's way for a number of reasons. The point is that we're not moral failures if we *don't*.

Killing and Letting Die

Philosopher James Rachels, in his 1975 article, "Active and Passive Euthanasia," made this distinction between *killing* and *letting die* to help motivate considerations about the morality of that practice. On Rachels's view, while there's clearly a *difference* between killing and letting die, it's far less clear that there's a *moral* difference between the two, despite what our gut may tell us.

In his account of active and passive euthanasia, Rachels asks us to imagine two scenarios. In the first, you administer a lethal dose of morphine, which renders the patient unconscious and then hastens her death. This is *active* euthanasia because you're doing something to bring about her death. It's also killing. In the second, you withhold treatments or—in what amounts to the same thing—you remove a patient from life support by "flipping the switch," and she dies as a result of starvation, dehydration, or system failure. This is *passive* euthanasia because you aren't doing anything to bring about her death. Instead, you're letting her die.

But, Rachels asks us to consider, what's the moral difference between injecting morphine and flipping a switch? To drive home his claim that there really isn't a moral difference, he gives another example through two cases:

> In the first case, Smith stands to gain a large inheritance if anything should happen to his six-year-old cousin. One evening while the child is taking his bath, Smith sneaks into the bathroom and drowns the child, and then arranges things so that it will look like an accident. In the second case, Jones also stands to gain if anything should happen to his six-year-old cousin. Like Smith, Jones sneaks in planning to drown the child in his bath. However, just as he enters the bathroom Jones sees the child slip and hit his head, and fall face down in the water. Jones is delighted; he

stands by, ready to push the child's head back under if it is necessary, but it is not necessary. With only a little thrashing about, the child drowns all by himself, "accidentally," as Jones watches and does nothing. Now Smith killed the child, whereas Jones "merely" let the child die. That is the only difference between them. Did either man behave better, from a moral point of view?

It's hard to see a moral difference between the two drowning cases, and yet they're exactly analogous, Rachels argues, to the two euthanasia cases. And, by analogy, pulling the lever and pushing the Fat Man aren't really morally different.

Organ-izational Restructuring

While the case of euthanasia isn't a trolley-type scenario, since it only involves one person whom we either kill or let die, we can combine trolley-type and medical ethics cases. Philosopher Judith Jarvis Thomson gives the following example in her 1985 essay "The Trolley Problem":

A brilliant transplant surgeon has five patients, each in need of a different organ, each of whom will die without that organ. Unfortunately, there are no organs available to perform any of these five transplant operations. A healthy young traveler, just passing through the city the doctor works in, comes in for a routine checkup. In the course of doing the checkup, the doctor discovers that his organs are compatible with all five of his dying patients. Suppose further that if the young man were to disappear, no one would suspect the doctor. Do you support the morality of the doctor to kill that tourist and provide his healthy organs to those five dying persons and save their lives?

This example is even more intimate than the Fat Man because you aren't just pushing some dude off a bridge— you're putting your surgical specialty to expert use in taking the blade to this fellow. Of course, he'll need to be prepped appropriately under full anesthesia during the surgery, so he won't feel a thing. That means you're at least off the hook for torturing him! But, if you know he'll die as a result of the surgeries, then why not just euthanize him at the start? After all, if we follow Rachels, there's no *moral* difference between active and passive euthanasia, between killing and letting die. Moreover, doctors have given an oath to do as little harm as possible in their practice, so it's hard to reduce this to a case in which his death is foreseen but unintended. Just kill the guy and harvest his organs! It's just a few more cc's of anesthesia, after all.

Collateral Damage or Collateral Murder?

It should strike no one as surprising that what we've said thus far presents us with a rather sticky moral quandary. If WikiLeaks releases a dump of unredacted documents, innocents may very well be put into harm's way, but if they *don't* release those documents, the illicit activities of powerful institutions remain secret and unchecked. Damned if you do; damned if you don't. Either way, though, it doesn't seem analogous to the Fat Man, because there's that moral distance. Pushing a button isn't the same, morally speaking, as pushing the Fat Man. And that moral distance affects our moral intuitions and sentiments and thus our moral decision-making.

We're probably all familiar with the banal expression of government doublespeak, "collateral damage." It's what we use to mask the often preventable and horrifying deaths of non-combatants in wartime maneuvers. To sound even more insensitive, we could call it "the cost of doing business." But, whatever we call it, we accept that there are times when such loss is inevitable or necessary in the service of counteracting a great evil in the world. And why is this? Because we know that we can't know all the conditions in any given situation. We always have *imperfect* information. We aren't omniscient. And, therefore, our decisions may result in *unforeseen* consequences. In the final analysis, then, we have to decide whether releasing damaging information—which may be damaging not only to those directly implicated but to otherwise innocent people—is worth the risk.

WikiLeaks released a video called "Collateral Murder," in which non-combatants are gunned down in an apparent case of collateral damage. Of course, the gunmen could have chosen not to fire on those individuals. Clearly, they had imperfect information, and we would like to think that, had they known who those individuals were, they would have held their fire. But, they didn't. Setting aside the motives of the gunmen who, like Adolf Eichmann, doubtless felt they were upholding their oath of enlistment and "just doing their job," these men actively targeted these individuals in their barrage. They believed (falsely) that these individuals were enemy combatants. In other words, they pushed the Fat Man. The gunmen intentionally took the lives of innocent human beings. At that level of analysis, these casualties aren't collateral *damage*; they're collateral *murder*.

It's hard to imagine anyone reasonably thinking otherwise, even if their actions are ultimately excused through the legal process that serves as the path for justice being rendered, and they receive no punishment for their actions. Those actions may ultimately be excused because the soldiers were operating under imperfect information about their targets: because they falsely believed their targets were enemy combatants, they acted; but, had they *known* that those individuals were *not* enemy combatants, they would have held their fire.

This lack of knowledge could constitute an excusing condition for their actions. Of course, the prosecution could argue that that very lack of information was sufficient reason for the soldiers to hold their fire. It's a case of the certainty of taking life versus the uncertainty of which lives are being taken. In other words, we don't know that these individuals have done anything wrong.

That's not the case with WikiLeaks.

WikiLevering

The fundamental question, then, is whether pulling the lever, and by analogy clicking the button releasing the information which may harm innocents, is morally prefer-able to doing nothing, which leaves the grave injustices and corrupt activities of powerful institutions secret and unaccountable.

Of course, in the real world, our knowledge is limited. We don't know, for example, that anyone *at all* will be harmed by the release of these documents, much less anyone who is properly considered an innocent. Such *epistemic uncertainty* has a way of ameliorating the difficulties of the decision. Because we can't know that real harm will come to innocent individuals, but we *do* know that the institutions implicated in the documents have acted in morally reprehensible ways, it becomes a matter of justice that we expose these actions *even if* there's the possibility of great harm to others. This is one step removed from the doctrine of double effect because the harm, while possible, isn't something that can be foreseen but unintended. We simply *can't* foresee the harm.

Think about the variations on the Trolley Problem we've looked at. In the original scenario, the single individual down the diversion track dies. In the Fat Man scenario, the fat man dies. In the similar thought experiments of Foot, the individual framed for the crime dies, is executed to quell the masses. And in the example of the organ transplants, the organ donor dies. In *every* case, two things are given: the single individual dies *and* we foresee this outcome.

The case of collateral murder is even clearer.

In the case of releasing information via WikiLeaks, we're left with a situation in which we know that grave injustice has been perpetrated, but we don't know what harm, if any, will result from bringing that injustice to light. In a situation such as that, we have an obligation to fight the injustice.

Do Your Duty

Immanuel Kant (1724–1804) famously argued that, in deter-mining whether an action has moral worth and thus whether it's our duty to perform it, we should pay no attention to the consequences that may (or may not) result from our action.

An action is morally right if and only if it conforms to a universalizable principle. In its most accessible form, that principle instructs us to treat the humanity of others always as an end in itself and never merely as a means to some other end. Kant puts it this way:

> Act in such a way that you treat humanity, whether in your own person or in the person of another, always at the same time as an end and never simply as a means.

This means that we're not allowed to pull the lever or push the Fat Man, nor kill a person to harvest his organs to save five other lives. Even if we don't intend their deaths, we are using them merely as a means to save the others. In other words, their life isn't worth anything more than a way to spare the lives of others.

In the case where we *know* that someone will die, we have a reason not to pull the lever (or push the Fat Man). Because we know they will die, our action fails to treat their humanity as an end in itself, turning it into a mere means to prevent the deaths of others. But, in cases where we lack the knowledge that someone will die, the *possibility* that they will die needs to be weighed against the morality of the action in question. If we know that the action in question is morally objectionable, then we have a duty to do something about it. And, if our motive for acting is to do our duty, as Kant says it must be to be a morally justified action, then the possibility of harm, even death, is outweighed by the fact that we're required by duty to attempt to rectify the known moral wrong. To put a point on it, if we know an action is morally wrong, then it's our duty to report it *even if* doing so means that harm to others is *possible*.

If we're tempted to consider releasing sensitive information about corrupt, unjust, and immoral actions as a *duty*, it's important to understand what type of duty it is. Kant offers two types of duties, based on what can reasonably be expected of a moral agent's capacity to fulfill them. He calls them *perfect* duties and *imperfect* duties. Perfect duties are those which we're obligated to fulfill *without exception*, for example the duty not to lie. It's *never* morally permissible to lie.

Imperfect duties, however, have a flexible quality to them, for example, the duty to help others. While we *are* obligated to help others, who, when, where and to what degree we have such an obligation create a less definite response. While we can always—in every case—refrain from lying, we simply can't do that when helping others. We *must* pick and choose. Is withholding information for the sake of saving lives the same as lying? What if releasing that information can actually save lives, while doing nothing will cost lives? What if releasing redacted information leads to uncertainty in our response, resulting in *other* lives or even *more* lives lost? It's a calculated risk no matter what we choose. In these cases, our duties would be *imperfect*.

Releasing information that implicates powerful institutions in corrupt and unjust activities, however, falls under *perfect* duty. We *know* these are morally wrong, unjust activities. Since ought implies can, meaning we can only have an obligation, or duty, under conditions in which we can keep it, in those cases where we're not able to release such information, we don't have the moral obligation to do so. But, in *every* case where we can, we ought to.

Kill Switch Engage

What the trolley needs is a *kill switch*, a safety mechanism used to shut off machinery in an emergency, when it can't be shut down in the usual manner. A kill switch is designed to shut down operation as quickly as possible, even if it damages the equipment, and to be operated simply and quickly, so that even a panicked operator or even a bystander can activate it. Such a modification *totally* changes the Trolley Problem thought experiment.

In the case of the WikiLeaking Problem, the kill switch *is* the computer mouse. The runaway trolley represents the powerful out of control institutions whose bureaucratic inertia puts the well-being of both ordinary individuals and the ideals of freedom, accountability, and transparency in jeopardy. By not throwing the switch—even given the possibility of harm—the information that's vital to exposing the corruption and illicit behavior of these powerful institutions remains intact, hidden from public moral and legal scrutiny.

In other words, we're allowing *known* injustice to continue unaddressed in an effort to avoid *unknown* harm to innocents. But, our duty is to act to correct the known injustice; we can't have a duty to prevent unknown harm, because such a duty would yield *moral paralysis*. Because we can't know what is unknown, and all actions have unknown consequences, we simply couldn't act morally in cases where there's a duty to prevent unknown harm. We can, however, act to rectify known injustice, and in fact have a duty to do so.

So, there you are, sitting at your computer, one click away from dropping a trove of classified documents that exposes the corruption, deception, and illicit behavior of some of the most powerful institutions in the world. If you click that button, the information will become available to anyone with access to the Internet, and the truth will be set free.

Engage!

References

Arendt, Hannah. 1972. *Crises of the Republic*. Harvest.
———. 2006 [1963]. *Eichmann in Jersusalem: A Report on the Banality of Evil*. Penguin.
Aristotle. 1999. *Nicomachean Ethics*. Hackett.
Assange, Julian. 2007. Conspiracy as Governance.
    <http://web.archive.org/web/20070129125831/http://iq.org:80/conspiracies.pdf>.
———. 2007. The Non-Linear Effects of Leaks on Unjust Systems of Governance.
    <http://web.archive.org/web/20071020051936/http://iq.org/#Thenonlineareffectsofleaksonunjustsystemsofgovernance>.
Baudrillard, Jean. 1993. *Symbolic Exchange and Death*. Sage.
Bentham , Jeremy. 2007 [1789]. *An Introduction to the Principles of Morals and Legislation*. Dover.
Berenson, Tessa. 2017. James Comey: WikiLeaks Is "Intelligence Porn," Not Journalism. *Time* (May 3rd)
    <http://time.com/4765358/fbi-james-comey-hearing-WikiLeaks>.
Blake, Aaron. 2016. Here Are the Latest, Most Damaging Things in the DNC's Leaked Emails. *Washington Post* (July 25th).
Brunton, Finn. 2011. Keyspace: WikiLeaks and the Assange Papers. *Radical Philosophy* 166 (March–April).
Charlie Rose TV show. Laura Poitras. *Charlie Rose*. <https://charlierose.com/videos/30538>.
Clinton, Hillary Rodham. 2017. *What Happened*. Simon and Schuster.
Collingwood, Robin G. 1940. *An Essay on Metaphysics*. Clarendon.

Cottingham, John. 2009. What Is Humane Philosophy and Why Is It at Risk? In A. O'Hare, ed., *Conceptions of Philosophy*. Royal Institute of Philosophy Supplement 65. Cambridge University Press.

Dewey, John. 2016. *The Public and Its Problems: An Essay in Political Inquiry*. Swallow Press.

Detmer, David. 2008. *Sartre Explained: From Bad Faith to Authenticity*. Open Court.

Deleuze, Gilles. 1995 [1968]. *Difference and Repetition*. Columbia University Press.

Domscheit-Berg, Daniel. 2011. *Inside WikiLeaks: My Time with Julian Assange at the World's Most Dangerous Website*. Cape.

Dworkin, Ronald. 1978. Civil Disobedience. In Dworkin, *Taking Rights Seriously*. Harvard University Press.

emptywheel. 2017. Why Accuracy about WikiLeaks Matters. <www.emptywheel.net/2017/05/07/why-accuracy-about-wikileaks-matters>.

Epicurus. 2012. *The Art of Happiness*. Penguin.

Erwin, Marshall, and Amy Belasco. 2003. *Intelligence Spending and Appropriations: Issues for Congress*. Congressional Research Service <http://fas.org/sgp/crs/intel/R42061.pdf>.

Foot, Philippa. 1967. The Problem of Abortion and the Doctrine of the Double Effect. *Oxford Review* 5.

Forbes, Patrick, dir. 2011 *WikiLeaks: Secrets and Lies*. Oxford Film and Television.

Frankfurt, Harry G. 2005. *On Bullshit*. Princeton University Press.

Gibney, Alex, dir. 2013. DVD. *We Steal Secrets: The Story of WikiLeaks*. Universal Studios Home Entertainment.

Glazer, Myron Peretz, and Penina Migdal Glazer. 1989. *The Whistle-Blowers: Exposing Corruption in Government and Industry*. Basic Books.

Goldsmith, Jack. 2017. Journalism in the Doxing Era: Is WikiLeaks Different from the *New York Times*? <www.lawfare-blog.com/journalism-doxing-era-WikiLeaks-different-new-york-times>.

Habermas, Jürgen. 1985. Civil Disobedience: Litmus Test for the Democratic Constitutional State. *Berkeley Journal of Sociology* 30.

Halchin, Elaine, and Frederick Kaiser. 2012. *Congressional Oversight of Intelligence: Current Structure and Alternatives*.

References

<http://digital.library.unt.edu/ark:/67531/metadc84042/m1/1/
high_res_d/RL32525_2012Mar26.pdf>.

Halpern, Sue. 2017. The Nihilism of Julian Assange. *New York
Review of Books* (July 13th).

Hampshire, Stuart. 1978. Public and Private Morality. In
Hampshire, ed., *Public and Private Morality*. Cambridge
University Press.

Holiday, Ryan. 2014. *The Obstacle Is the Way: The Timeless Art of
Turning Trials into Triumph*. Portfolio.

I Am WikiLeaks Legal Defence Fund. 2017. Open Letter to
President Trump. <www.iamWikiLeaks.org/openletter>.

Iglesias, Pablo. 2001–02. Desobediencia civil y movimiento
antiglobalización. Una herramienta de intervención política.
Revista Telemática de Filosofía del Derecho.

ITV. 2016. Assange on Peston on Sunday: "More Clinton Leaks to
Come" <www.itv.com/news/update/2016-06-12/assange-on-
peston-on-sunday-more-clinton-leaks-to-come>.

Johnson, Roberta Ann. 2003. *Whistle-Blowing: When It Works—
and Why*. Lynne Rienner.

Kant, Immanuel. 1983. *Perpetual Peace and Other Essays on
Politics, History, and Morals*. Hackett.

———. 2002. *Groundwork for the Metaphysics of Morals*. Oxford
University Press.

Khan, Jemima. 2013. Jemima Khan on Julian Assange: How the
Wikileaks Founder Alienated His Allies. <www.newstatesman
.com/2013/02/jemima-khan-julian-assange-how-wikileaks-
founder-alienated-his-allies>.

Leigh, David, and Luke Harding. 2011. *WikiLeaks: Inside Julian
Assange's War on Secrecy*. Public Affairs.

Leonhardt, David. 2017. A French Lesson for the American
Media. *New York Times* (May 9th).

Machiavelli, Niccolò. 1995. *The Prince*. Hackett.

McIntyre, Alison. 2014. Doctrine of Double Effect. *The Stanford
Encyclopedia of Philosophy* (Winter 2014) <https://plato
.stanford.edu/archives/win2014/entries/double-effect>.

Malloggi, Francesca. 2017. The Value of Privacy for Social Relationships." *Social Epistemology Review and Reply Collective* 6:2.

Mangan, Joseph T. *An Historical Analysis of the Principle of
Double Effect*. https://philarchive.org/archive/MANAHA-2

Mann, Michael E., Raymond S. Bradley, and Malcolm K. Hughes.
1998. Global-scale Temperature Patterns and Climate
Forcing over the Past Six Centuries. *Nature* 392.

References

Manne, Robert. 2015 [2011]. *Cypherpunk Revolutionary: On Julian Assange*. Schwartz.

McLaughlin, Jenna. 2015. Laura Poitras Sues U.S. Government to Find Out Why She Was Repeatedly Stopped at the Border. *The Intercept* (July 13th) <https://theintercept.com/2015/07/13/laura-poitras-sues-u-s-government-find-repeatedly-stopped-border>.

Mill, John Stuart. 2002. *Utilitarianism*. Hackett.

Milton's John. 2016 [1644]. *Areopagitica and Other Writings*. Penguin.

Moore, Tim. 2013. Critical Thinking: Seven Definitions in Search of a Concept. *Studies in Higher Education* 38:4.

National Commission on Terrrorist Attacks upon the United States. 2004. *The 9-11 Commission Report*. Norton. <http://9-11commission.gov/report>.

Nietzsche, Friedrich. 1980. *On the Advantage and Disadvantage of History for Life*. Hackett.

O'Sullivan, Patrick, and Ola Ngau 2014. *Business Ethics: A European Review* 23:4 <http://libproxy.redeemer.ca:2048/login?url=http://search.ebscohost.com/login.aspx?direct=true&db=bsh&AN=97982092&site=eds-live>.

Padilla, Margarita. 2012. *El kit de la lucha en Internet: Para viejos militantes y nuevas activistas*. Madrid: Traficantes de Sueños.

Peters, Douglas P., and Stephen J. Ceci. 1980. A Manuscript Masquerade. *The Sciences* 20:7.

Plato. 2002. *Five Dialogues: Euthyphro, Apology, Crito, Meno, Phaido*. Hackett.

Poitras, Laura. dir. 2017. *Risk*. DVD. Virgil Films and Entertainment.

Rachels, James. 1975. Active and Passive Euthanasia. *New England Journal of Medicine* 292.

Rawls, John. 1999. *A Theory of Justice*. Harvard University Press.

Rosenbach, Eric, and Aki Peritz. 2009. *Confrontation or Collaboration? Congress and the Intelligence Community*. Kennedy School of Government <http://belfercenter.org>.

Rosenblum, Nancy L. 1081. Thoreau's Militant Conscience. *Political Theory* 9:1.

Sartre, Jean-Paul. 1955. *No Exit and Three Other Plays: Dirty Hands, The Flies, and The Respectful Prostitute*. Vintage.

———. 1956 [1943]. *Being and Nothingness: A Phenomenological Essay on Ontology*. Simon and Schuster.

References

Savickey, Beth. 2016. Wittgenstein's Slapstick. *Performance Philosophy Journal* 2:1.

Scheuerman, William E. 2014. Whistleblowing as Civil Disobedience: The Case of Edward Snowden. *Philosophy and Social Criticism* 40:7.

Scott, Mark. 2017. U.S. Far-Right Activists Promote Hacking Attack Against Macron. <https://www.nytimes.com/2017/05/06/world/europe/emmanuel-macron-hack-french-election-marine-le-pen.html>.

Society of Professional Journalists. 2014. SPJ Code of Ethics. <www.spj.org/ethicscode.asp>.

Susskind, Leonard. 2008. *The Black Hole War: My Battle with Stephen Hawking to Make the World Safe for Quantum Mechanics*. Little, Brown.

Taylor, Carrie Ann, ed. 2018. *The Ethics of WikiLeaks*. Greenhaven.

Thomson, Judith Jarvis. 1985. The Trolley Problem. *Yale Law Journal* 94.

Thoreau, Henry David. 1996. *Thoreau: Political Writings*. Cambridge University Press.

United Nations. 2017. Universal Declaration of Human Rights. <www.un.org/en/universal-declaration-human-rights>.

United States South District Court, Southern District of Florida. 2017. Transcript of Motion Hearing had before the Honorable William J. Zloch, United States District Judge, April 25, 2017. <http://jampac.us/wp-content/uploads/2016/07/042517cw2.pdf>.

Walzer, Michael. 1973. Political Action: The Problem of Dirty Hands. *Philosophy and Public Affairs* 2:2.

WikiLeaks. 2010. Collateral Murder. <https://collateralmurder.wikileaks.org>.

WikiLeaks. 2017. About: What Is WikiLeaks? <https://WikiLeaks.org/About.html>.

WikiLeaks. 2017. Macron Campaign Emails. <https://wikileaks.org/macron-emails>.

Winterbotham, Frederick. 1974. *The Ultra Secret*. Harper and Row.

Wray, Stefan. 1998. Electronic Civil Disobedience and the World Wide Web of Hacktivism: A Mapping of Extraparliamentarian Direct Action Net Politics. *Switch* 4:2.

Zafra, Remedios. 2012. *A Connected Room of One's Own*. Fórcola.

Partners

LESLIE A. AARONS is an associate professor of philosophy at the City University of New York. She has published numerous book chapters and articles in both Public Philosophy and Environmental Ethics. She is presently writing a book engaging these two philosophical specializations.

ROBERT ARP teaches philosophy and works as a research instructor for the US Army. He has published articles, book chapters, and books in several areas of philosophy. Most recently, he co-authored *Philosophy Hacks: Shortcuts to 100 Ideas* (2018) and co-edited *Bad Arguments: 100 of the Most Important Fallacies in Western Philosophy* (2018).

JENNIFER BAKER teaches philosophy and ethics at the College of Charleston. She works on virtue ethics and attempts to update the ancient approaches for use today. She has co-edited *Economics and the Virtues: Building a New Moral Foundation* (2016) and has a forthcoming book on how a Stoic would think about ethics in business.

ADAM BARKMAN (PhD, Free University of Amsterdam) is Professor of Philosophy and Chair of the Philosophy Department at Redeemer University College. He is the author or co-editor of a dozen books, most recently *A Critical Companion to James Cameron* (2018).

AZEEM CHAUDRY received his JD from Rutgers Law School in 2016 and has interests in ethics, philosophy of law, and philosophy of information.

MARLENE CLARK teaches courses filled with literature, film, art, and philosophy in the Division of Interdisciplinary Studies at the City College of New York, CUNY. She is currently working on a book concerning the six numbered Women paintings of Willem de Kooning.

LOUIS COLOMBO is a professor of philosophy at Bethune-Cookman University in Daytona Beach, where he teaches courses in Ethics and the history of Western Philosophy. His research interests include Hegel, Critical Theory, and American Pragmatism, although living and teaching in sunny Florida makes the call of the beach almost irresistible.

CHRISTIAN COTTON is an independent scholar and freelance writer who has taught philosophy and religion at the University of Georgia and Piedmont College. He has published chapters in *Homeland and Philosophy* (2014), *Justified and Philosophy* (2015), and *Bad Arguments: 100 of the Most Important Fallacies in Western Philosophy* (2018).

KIMBERLY S. ENGELS is Assistant Professor of Philosophy at Molloy College in Rockville Centre New York. She has published articles and book chapters in several areas of philosophy, including in the application of Jean-Paul Sartre's work to issues in contemporary life. Most recently, she co-edited a book on the television show *Westworld* and philosophy.

DANIEL CLARKSON FISHER is a writer whose work has appeared in AlterNet, *New Politics*, PopMatters, *Bright Lights Film Journal*, Nonfics, *Tricycle*, Religion Dispatches, and *Diabolique*, among other publications. He has taught for Hartford Seminary, Antioch Education Abroad, and University of the West, and is currently a student in the Master of Fine Arts in Documentary Media program at Ryerson University.

JOSHUA HAUTALA is an independent scholar interested in the intersection of philosophy and politics, in particular, issues relating to Native American interests and rights.

CHRISTOPHER KETCHAM teaches Business and Ethics at the University of Houston—Downtown. He does research in risk management, applied ethics, and social justice.

DAVID LAROCCA <www.davidlarocca.org> has edited three books on film and media: *The Philosophy of Charlie Kaufman* (2011), *The Philosophy of War Films* (2014), and *The Philosophy of Documentary Film: Image, Sound, Fiction, Truth* (2016).

PETER LUDLOW is an American philosopher of language. He is noted for interdisciplinary work at the interface of linguistics and philosophy—in particular on the philosophical foundations of Noam Chomsky's theory of generative linguistics and on the foundations of the theory of meaning in linguistic semantics.

TRIP MCCROSSIN is Assistant Teaching Professor in the Department of Philosophy at Rutgers University. He has interests in ethics, political philosophy, and evil. He is co-editing *Blade Runner 2049 and Philosophy* (2019).

DAN MIORI is a physician assistant and clinical adjunct faculty member at the SUNY Buffalo School of Biomedical Science where he teaches clinical ethics. He has contributed chapters to several philosophy and popular culture books but is still waiting for that big break.

ISADORA MOSCH is a Lecturer of Philosophy at Georgia College and State University. She has published articles and presented at academic conferences in several areas of philosophy, including Philosophy of Emotion, Ethics, Feminism, and Pop Culture. She has written on philosophy of humor in *Philosophy Now* and most recently, she was the Keynote Speaker at Mercer University's Philosophy Colloquium.

MIQUEL COMAS OLIVER, *Praxis* research group collaborator (University of the Balearic Islands, Spain <http://praxis.uib.eu /Equip>) has published in political philosophy and Critical Theory, especially on civil disobedience and the transparency principle. He authored *Disobedient Intersubjectivity in Hannah Arendt: Neither Solitary Heroes nor Rebellious Masses* (in Spanish) and co-edited *Technocriticism: The Crossroads between Technology and Social Movements* (in Catalan).

BRAD PATTY is Senior Vice President for Research and Analysis at the Security Studies Group. From 2007 to 2009, Dr. Patty advised US Army units in Iraq on tribal affairs and information as part of more than a decade's involvement in America's wars. He won the Metaphysical Society of America's Aristotle Prize in 2014, and has received formal commendations from the 1st Cavalry Division, 3rd Infantry Division, 2/1 Armored Division, and 30th Heavy Brigade.

L. BROOKE RUDOW-ABOUHARB is a lecturer in philosophy at Georgia College and State University. Her research focuses primarily on issues within political philosophy, feminist philosophy, and environmental ethics. Some of her publications include "Creating Life, Giving Birth, and Learning to Die" in the volume *Philosophical Inquiries into Pregnancy, Childbirth, and Mothering*, "Tragedy and Reconciliation in the Ramayana" in the *Journal for Indian Philosophy and Religion*, and "Dismantling Purity: Toward a Feminist Curdling of Hawaiian Identity" in the *Feminist Philosophy Quarterly*.

FRANK SCALAMBRINO teaches philosophy in Colorado Springs. He has published numerous articles and books, including *Living in the Light of Death: Existential Philosophy in the Eastern Tradition, Zen, Samurai, and Haiku* (2017) and *Full Throttle Heart: Nietzsche, Either/Or* (2015).

ROBERT F.J. SEDDON received his PhD in Philosophy from the University of Durham, where he retains an Honorary Fellowship in the Department of Philosophy and membership of the Centre for the Ethics of Cultural Heritage. His interests incline towards ethics broadly construed, and the ethics of cultural heritage in particular.

Index

1984

AND PHILOSOPHY
IS RESISTANCE FUTILE?

EDITED BY EZIO DI NUCCI AND STEFAN STORRIE